The
PERFECT
COMPANION

*Understanding, Training &
Bonding with Your Dog!*

Karen Davison

ISBN-13: 978-1475235296

Dedication

This book is dedicated to the owners that I have enjoyed working with over the years and all the dogs that have helped me to become a better trainer!

- -

TABLE OF CONTENTS

A DOG'S PRAYER

Treat me kindly my beloved master, for no heart in all the world is more grateful for kindness than the loving heart of me.

Do not break my spirit with a stick, or though I should lick your hand between the blows, your patience and understanding will more quickly teach me the things you would have me do.

Speak to me often, for your voice is the world's sweetest music, as you must know by the fierce wagging of my tail when your footstep falls upon my waiting ear.

When it is cold and wet, please take me inside...for I am now a domesticated animal, no longer used to bitter elements...and I ask no greater glory than the privilege of sitting at your feet beside the hearth...though had you no home, I would rather follow you through ice and snow than rest upon the softest pillow in the warmest home in all the land...for you are my god...and I am your devoted worshiper.

Keep my pan filled with fresh water, for although I should not reproach you were it dry. I cannot tell you when I suffer thirst.

Feed me clean food, that I may stay well, to romp and play and do your bidding, to walk by your side, and stand ready, willing and able to protect you with my life, should your life be in danger.

And, beloved master, should the Great Master see fit to deprive me of my health or sight, do not turn me away from you. Rather hold me gently in your arms as skilled hands grant me the merciful boon of eternal rest...and I will leave you knowing with the last breath I drew, my fate was ever safest in your hands.

By Beth Norman Harris 1948

INTRODUCTION

Why is it that so many of us choose to share our lives with dogs?

Dog hair floating in your coffee, the inevitable slob and dirt up the walls, having to pick up their poo...

To the uninitiated this may seem like a lot of bother, but it is a small price to pay for the joy and companionship dogs can offer us.

The void of language between our two species leaves space for a deeper more intuitive connection. At times dogs seem more sensitive to our needs and emotions than our fellow human beings. They accept us without judgement, on hand to cheer us up when we are having a bad day or comfort us when we are sad or ill.

Owning a dog is a joy, if we base our relationship on trust, consistency and a positive approach we gain a devoted and loyal companion that brings something unique and rewarding to our lives.

This publication is much more than a training manual; it explores the inner workings of the dog's mind to give you a real understanding of how and why positive reinforcement gains the best and most reliable results. From a detailed puppy socialisation program to environmental enrichment and suggested activities and games that will build confidence, give your dog a happy fulfilled life and strengthen the bond between you, laying the foundation for a strong and rewarding relationship.

You will find detailed step by step instructions on how to teach basic commands using various different positive training techniques, so that you can choose the method that best suits you and your dog.

It encourages you to consider your dog's natural behaviour and to channel their instincts into positive activities and reveals why stimulating your dog's mind has many behavioural and physical benefits, possibly contributing to longevity.

Some common behavioural issues are covered in detail, explaining the causes, prevention and solutions, as well as a general problem solving guide, with a checklist to help you diagnose the root cause of problems and suggests what action may be needed, in order to resolve them.

The Perfect Companion, Understanding, Training and Bonding with your Dog! Written by professional dog trainer and canine behaviourist Karen Davison, is essential reading for all new puppy owners and a valuable source of information for those of us who want to get the best out of our relationship with man's best friend.

SECTION 1

HELP YOUR PUPPY GROW INTO A CONFIDENT ADULT

Puppy Development

Detailed Socialisation Program

House Training

Feeding Regimes and Diet

Realistic Expectations

Picking up the signals

Setting up the environment

Effective Clean up

PUPPY DEVELOPMENT

The early stages of development have the greatest influence on temperament and learning ability. Experiences gained (both positive and negative) during this period will have a lasting effect on your dog's ability to interact with people and other species and determines how well your dog will cope with everyday life. The first three months are when rapid learning and development occurs.

4 - 7 Weeks -

It is this stage when puppies learn and practice their canine social skills through education by the Dam and intensive play with each other. Play is an important mould to adult social behaviour.

Play between littermates and interaction with their mother is crucial in the learning process. It teaches communication skills, inhibited bite and greeting rituals which are vitally important when interacting with other dogs in later life.

These early interactions promote communal behaviour and social bonding and helps puppies to improve coordination, physical dexterity and problem solving, thus accelerating experience.

Play between dogs is a natural, useful and enjoyable activity and puppies that are allowed to partake in a normal period of canine socialisation, will continue to partake in and enjoy play throughout the course of their adult lives.

Puppies that are removed from the litter too early, are likely to have poor social skills, become fearful, inhibited or over reactive/aggressive when they meet other dogs.

It is important therefore, that puppies should remain with the litter for a minimum of 8 weeks.

4 - 12 Weeks -

During this time puppies respond to external stimulus and will actively explore their environment. It is important to give them different objects and textures to explore at this stage and introduce new experiences. Puppies that are handled often during early stages of development will be more confident with people.

During this crucial stage of development, everything that your puppy comes in to contact with will make a lasting impression. It is important that your puppy is exposed to as many different positive experiences as possible.

At this stage your puppy will learn how to interact with people, other species and new environments. Socialising with small animals and other species is especially important for dogs that have a strong prey drive and for dogs living in rural areas, it is during this stage that controlled exposure to livestock should be introduced.

Puppies that are raised in a sensory rich and interesting environment, will be able to cope much better, will be well adjusted and balanced, suffer less stress, will have good problem solving skills and more confidence.

It has been shown that puppies that are reared in a limited environment can develop impaired learning ability, hyperactivity and fearfulness. Thus the wider the range of exposure to different sights, sounds and smells, the more confident the mature dog will be.

12 weeks and beyond

This is the third and final stage in the process of growth and development. Unlike the first two stages it has no time limit and by comparison covers a very long period of time.

During this time the positive sum or experiences has a cumulative effect on the individual. The more you can exposure your dog to a wide variety of interesting, novel and exciting experiences with regular opportunities to freely investigate, manipulate and interact, the better.

SOCIALISATION

Good socialisation is important to help your puppy grow into a well adjusted, well behaved and confident adult.

In this section you will find suggestions for a socialisation program with explanations of the benefits of each element.

People

Invite people of all ages and both genders to visit and encourage them to greet your puppy only when s/he has got over their initial excitement.

It is important to supervise and encourage children in gentle handling as a bad experience at this point, may cause nervousness and fear biting toward children. Strict adult supervision is essential at all times.

This will build confidence and prevent nervousness with unfamiliar people.

Not interacting with the pup until he/she is calm, will help to prevent overzealous greeting behaviour.

Exposing to children of all ages will help your puppy get used to the noisy and sometimes unpredictable nature of children in a safe environment.

Stimulating Environment

Provide an interesting and stimulating environment. Cardboard boxes add interest; different types, sizes, shapes and texture of toys as well as obstacles to climb and explore. Change regularly.

Let your puppy experience different types and textures of flooring.

This will encourage your puppy to explore his surroundings and build confidence when faced with new experiences.

Helps develop coordination and physical dexterity.

Continued Socialisation with Animals

Allow your puppy to interact with other vaccinated dogs of all sizes and ages and introduce to other species. This should be done in a controlled environment and under strict supervision. As with children, it is important to make these experiences positive.

This will encourage continued sociability and develop correct approach/interaction with different species.

Help to reduce prey drive responses.

Feeding

Encourage all family members to feed your puppy. Keep a small portion of food back and add to the dish while the puppy is eating.

This will prevent food aggression/resource guarding.

NEVER take food away from your puppy, always add food while they are eating.

Grooming/Examination

When your puppy is tired and relaxed, rub down gently with a towel and introduce to grooming. Just a few strokes of the brush to begin with. If your puppy is inclined to bite the brush, give them something positive to occupy them as a distraction.

Begin basic examination - check and handle ears, lift the lips to look at their teeth, handle the tail and feet, check their pads, nails and webbing between their toes. Once the puppy is happy to accept this type of handling, ask other people to do the same.

This will get your puppy accustomed to being groomed and dried and used to general handling and stress free nail clipping.

Veterinary examination will be less traumatic for your dog and much easier for your vet!

Travel

Take your puppy out for short car rides.

As the inner ear is not fully developed, puppies can suffer from motion sickness. It is important therefore to keep trips very short to begin with, just a few minutes out and back.

- -

This will get your puppy used to car travel and allow him/her to observe the outside world.

By keeping the trips short, it will help to prevent feelings of nausea which can form a negative association with going out in the car.

Positive Controlled Separation

Making sure you use a safe room (i.e no chewable wires etc) leave your puppy alone with toys and safe chew items for very short periods of time, gradually increase the time that s/he is left alone. If your puppy gets distressed, try using a baby gate so that they can still see you. Leave a radio on in the room and try not to respond to vocalisation during this alone time and where possible wait until they are quiet (even if it is only for a few seconds) before letting them out.

This will get your puppy used to being left alone and prevent the development of separation anxiety.

Visiting your Vet

Take your puppy in to visit your veterinary practice before their first appointment for vaccinations.

Keep your puppy in your arms to prevent any risks of exposure to disease and ask your vet and support staff to make a fuss of your puppy and give a few treats. This should be an ongoing event even as your dog matures. Whenever you are passing the practice with your dog, pop in for a few minutes of positive interaction.

If your dog only goes to the vet for treatment, they will form negative associations and can become very stressed each time you have a veterinary appointment.

Positive interactions with the vet and support staff will take the trauma out of the situation when you do need to take them in for treatment.

Varied Walks

When the full course of vaccinations are complete, allow your puppy to explore as many different environments as possible, starting with quieter locations and progressing gradually to busier places. Country locations where they may see livestock, forest, beaches and lakes, playgrounds and town parks, dog shows and country fairs, car parks and shopping centres. Get your puppy used to traffic on very quiet roads and move up to busier locations gradually.

Exposing your puppy to different environments will build confidence, supply interest and mental stimulation.

Continued Interaction and Socialisation

When out and about allow your puppy to interact with other dogs. It is best not to let them meet and greet every dog, choose carefully the dogs that you allow them to interact with. You want experiences to be positive. Always ask the other owner if their dog is friendly with other dogs and ask permission to let them greet each other. Check your local area for puppy training and socialisation classes (making sure that the trainer is qualified and uses positive reinforcement methods)

Puppies begin to develop their social skills while still in the litter, it is important to allow them to continue to develop these interactions with different dogs. If you do not allow your dog to interact in this way, these skills can diminish and lead to fear and they can become over reactive and aggressive when meeting other dogs.

Controlling which dogs they are permitted to interact with will prevent bad experiences and teach your puppy that they can't interact with every dog they see.

Handling a Fear Response

Remember, your puppy has limited life experiences. Although puppies are inquisitive by nature, you may get a situation where they seem hesitant or afraid. It is quite normal for puppies to show an initial fear response to something new.

It is important that you do not react to this by making a fuss and trying to reassure your puppy, as this will reinforce the fear response, making it more likely to occur. Instead just observe your puppy, s/he should recover quite quickly and then move in to investigate. If your puppy does not recover however, reduce the stimulus to an acceptable level i.e. move further away from the object or situation to a distance that they can cope with.

Without force, work gradually closer in increments that your puppy can cope with, rewarding confident behaviour with positive reinforcement.

HOUSE TRAINING

With a positive approach house training is reasonably quick and easy. However if handled in a negative way, it may not only prevent success but can also cause a breakdown in the relationship between you and your dog, causing stress and anxiety in both parties.

The good news is, it is never too late to turn things around.

Whether you are trying to house train a puppy or an older dog the following tips will help you achieve success.

You will find detailed instruction on how to teach toileting on command in Section 4.

Feeding Regimes and Diet

When house training, try and have regular feeding times and use an appropriate high quality diet. Regular meals result in regular bowel movements. Avoid leaving food down because if dogs are allowed to graze all day, the will defecate all day as well. Food should only be left down for 10 minutes, if it hasn't been eaten by then, take it away until the next feed time.

Dogs usually need to move their bowels 10-30 minutes after eating if fed at consistent times but this can vary from dog to dog. It is a good idea to try and keep a record of the time after feeding that your dog eliminates, so that you can get an idea of the best times to take them outside.

Young puppies will need to be fed three times a day, their stomach capacity is small and so they need to eat little and often to acquire enough food for growth.

If your puppy is consistently having bowel movements overnight, try and adjust your feeding times so that they either have it done before they go to bed, or manage to hold it until morning.

This can take a little experimentation, and it is best to only adjust one feed time at a time, be sure to stick to it consistently for at least a week to allow things to settle into a routine to gauge whether it is having the desired result.

Food Quality

Another important aspect to the amount and frequency of defecation is the quality of the food. This is relevant to dogs of all ages.

If the food is high quality it will be more digestible and produce less waste. Low quality foods usually contain a lot of cheap filler ingredients, which are less digestible creating more frequent and unformed stools.

Realistic Expectations

Young puppies need time to develop the muscles that control bladder and bowel movements.

Do not expect your puppy to be able to hold these actions reliably for any length of time until they are 4-5 months of age. This varies depending on the individual dog.

Until such time as this is achieved you can expect to have to clean up after your puppy over night and also if you are leaving them unattended for a length of time during the day.

Older Dogs

You may be house training an older dog, often this is because they are a rescue and may have previously been an outdoor dog.

Usually training is much quicker with an adult dog, as they have much better control.

If your adult dog was previously clean in the house and begins to have accidents, the first port of call should be your vet. Urinary tract and bladder infections can cause these types of problems and some bitches, if they were neutered too early, can suffer from oestrogen deficient urinary incontinence (this is discussed in Section 7).

These types of problems are medical issues rather than behaviour problems and your vet will be able to prescribe appropriate medication to treat the problem.

Setting up the Environment

While your dog is under training, try and restrict access to a room that has a door leading outside, preferably with a washable floor. Always let your dog out of this door to go to the toilet.

If you know for certain that your puppy or dog has got all of their business out of the way, then it will be fairly safe to allow them access to other parts of the house providing they are under strict supervision.

You can purchase puppy training pads, but in my opinion they are expensive and too small to be effective.

In the training area, begin by covering a very large proportion of the floor with newspaper; (most newsagents will give old newspapers away for free) this should start at the door leading to outside, coming into the room.

If there is newspaper down, puppies will usually go onto it to eliminate. If your puppy is missing the paper, make the area larger.

Once your dog is consistently going on the paper, you can begin to gradually reduce the area, always working from the door into the room.

If at any time your puppy begins to miss the paper, go back a stage and increase the area of coverage again.

Progress, until you have only one sheet just inside the door, this should be done gradually over a period of time. The idea is that you will teach your dog to move toward the door, giving you a nice clear signal when they want to go to the toilet.

If you notice your puppy heading onto the paper, try and get them outside before they produce. If you missed the opportunity, always verbally praise them for going on the paper, but save the stronger reinforcement (more about this later) for when they go outside.

Remove soiled paper as soon as possible; do not forget to clean the floor thoroughly before replacing with fresh paper.

If it is a dry day, you can place soiled newspaper outside and weigh down with stones to prevent it blowing away. This encourages your dog by leaving the scent in an appropriate environment.

Picking up the Signals

The more frequently you can intervene and get your dog or puppy outside, the more opportunities you will have to reward them. Each success will help to make the behaviour (toileting outside) stronger.

Dogs will exhibit clear signals when they are about to go to the toilet. You need to be observant and tune in to these signals.

Commonly they will stop what they are doing, put their nose to the floor and begin to sniff; this is usually an indication that they are going to urinate. Older male dogs may scent higher up vertical surfaces, often turning a couple of times against the surface before lifting the leg. Circling usually indicates that they are going to have a bowel movement.

Pay particular attention if your dog goes to an area where they have previously soiled.

Distract them with an excited tone, hand clapping or sound distraction like a squeaky toy and encourage them to follow you outside.

If you have missed the opportunity and your dog has already squatted, try and recall what they were doing immediately before the action and watch for that behaviour in order to pre-empt it next time.

It is a good idea to set aside dedicated training sessions to teach them to follow you out to the garden so that when you do need to get them out, they understand what is expected.

This is achieved by associating a cue, for instance 'Lets Go', keep your tone light hearted and excited, go outside and use lots of encouragement. Reinforce them with a reward when they follow you out.

Success Breeds Success

The more you positively reinforce your dog for toileting outside, the better. It is important that you go out with your dog so that you are in a position to reward them as soon as they produce.

If behaviour is positively reinforced, it will become stronger and more likely to occur. In other words the more frequently you are successful, the more likely you are to achieve positive results. With this in mind try and get your puppy or dog outside at regular intervals.

You should take your dog out at regular intervals, particularly at key times: .

- ❖ When your dog or puppy has just woken up
- ❖ After a play session
- ❖ After eating or drinking

Try and ensure that they have 'emptied' before leaving them unattended during the day and before settling them down for the night.

Always make sure that you reward them for toileting when out for walks.

The Importance of Cleanup

Compared to dogs, our sense of smell is virtually non existent. To get an idea of how much more refined a dog's sense of smell is, we can compare the amount of scent receptors:-

- ❖ Humans - 5 Million
- ❖ Terriers -147 million
- ❖ German shepherd -225 million
- ❖ Bloodhounds - 300 million

To us, cleaning up with disinfectant appears to be effective, but dogs will still detect the odour of urine beneath strong smelling cleaners. Any trace of odour will encourage your dog to continue to mark on top of the same spot, therefore it is important to ensure all traces of odour are eliminated.

If your dog is inclined to repeatedly mark the same area, clean up thoroughly as outlined below; then place their crate, bed or food dish on the area to break the cycle of behaviour. Dogs will not usually soil where they eat or sleep.

Avoid cleaners with ammonia as this is one of the components in urine.

Hard Floors

To effectively remove the scent you will need an enzyme cleaner. Biological washing powder (not non-biological) is ideal but you can use any enzyme cleaner from the supermarket or pet shop. You will also need either white vinegar or surgical spirits.

Mix up a solution of the enzyme cleaner with warm water and thoroughly clean the area. Go over it with clean water and dry. Put either white vinegar or surgical spirits on kitchen paper towel and wipe over the area.

This will completely remove the scent. If you have a mature male, it may be necessary to clean vertical surfaces as well.

If using surgical spirits, make sure to test the application in an area out of sight to check that it will not cause any damage to the surface material. Although surgical spirits will leave a very strong 'surgical' smell, it evaporates quickly.

Carpets and Rugs

It is better to either restrict access to areas in the house that have carpets, or remove rugs until your dog is house trained as cleaning up and removing odours is a little more involved on these types of surfaces.

Avoid using steam cleaners as heat will bond the protein in the urine into man made fibres leaving a permanent stain and odour.

The quicker you clean up, the better. Use a good wad of kitchen paper towels to blot up the urine. Avoid rubbing action as this will only spread to a larger area. Keep replacing with clean towels until the majority has been absorbed. For rugs, place a wad of paper towel underneath during this process,

The next stage is to use a solution of 50% white vinegar to 50% water. Work this solution well into the carpet fibres using a brush. This will neutralise the ammonia. Repeat the blotting process as before until most of the moisture is lifted. Scrub the area with a solution of biological washing powder and warm water, blot once again and then sprinkle with baking soda and allow to dry. Vacuum thoroughly once dry.

For older stains this process may need to be repeated.

- -

SECTION 2

RE-EXAMINING DOMINANCE

The Origins of Pack Rule Theory

Dominance

Aggression

Dog Social Behaviour

Rank Reduction – The Truth

House Rules not Pack Rules

THE ORIGINS OF PACK RULE THEORY

Before exploring positive reinforcement training methods, it is important to explain why modern dog trainers no longer apply pack rule theory to train or modify dog behaviour.

You will often hear that you must be the 'alpha' or 'pack leader' to your dog. Sadly, the idea that you have to dominate your dog in order for them to obey and respect you is still widely promoted. But if we look at the facts logically, do they add up?

Where did the idea of pack leadership and alpha dominance first originate?

This theory was first developed many decades ago from early studies of wolf behaviour. At the time our understanding of wolf social behaviour was limited, it was thought that packs consisted of random groups of wolves that came together at the onset of winter in order to hunt large prey.

Wolves are elusive and difficult to study in the wild and so, in order to study their behaviour, ecologists gathered individual wolves from various zoos and put them together as a captive colony. When unrelated animals from any species are put together in these abnormal conditions, tension between individuals will often result in competitive aggression.

In this unnatural setting, a dominance hierarchy was caused, rather than revealed. This was then supposed to represent normal pack behaviour and the idea that packs had dominate alpha, subordinate beta and submissive omega members was first documented.

Our understanding of wolf behaviour has come a long way since these early studies and it is now recognised that wolf packs consist of family groups, usually a breeding pair and their offspring. Like any family group the parents guide, care for and teach their offspring, and they naturally follow.

Wolf biologists today do not refer to 'alpha' animals within a pack; rather they are referred to as the 'breeding' pair. All pack members contribute to the feeding and care of the offspring, including yearlings from the previous years mating.

Contrary to popular belief if food is scarce, breeding females and pups are fed first. When yearlings mature, they do not challenge the breeding pair for social dominance; rather they disperse looking for a mate of their own to form a new pack. The view of the pack as an aggressive assortment of wolves consistently competing with each other to take over the pack has no foundation in reality.

The social structure of the wolf pack is much more complex than the simple outdated view of the strict hierarchical society. In the old view, from which much of 'pack rule theory' for the domestic dog was developed, the alpha led with an iron paw, being entitled to privileges such as always eating first and getting the best food, always instigating social interactions, leading the pack from the front in travel and hunting etc. etc. Subordinate members attempting to take privileges above their station were dealt with swiftly and violently.

We can see today that this is clearly not the case. Life in the wild is fraught with danger; packs of wolves are non-violent family units that depend on each other for survival. Working together they are more likely to successfully bring down large prey and during hunting it is usually the lighter, faster animals that begin the hunt, testing and wearing down the prey and separating weaker animals from the herd. The larger and more experienced wolves come in at the end for the kill.

It is recognised that dogs and wolves share a common ancestry, but evolution and domestication over many thousands of years have changed dogs to such a large extent, that it is not reasonable to compare dog behaviour to the behaviour of the wolf, just as we wouldn't expect the study of monkeys to help us gain a deeper understanding of human behaviour.

If the model of a strict hierarchical society cannot be applied to wolves, how can it possibly be relevant to domestic dogs?

Dominance

If owners are experiencing training or behavioural problems with their dogs, is this due to a display of dominance?

People working along the line of pack rule theory believe that dogs are challenging the owner's authority and showing dominance if:-

❖ The dog ignores commands.

❖ The dog pulls on the lead.

❖ The dog won't come back when called.

In my experience these types of issues show a lack of, or inconsistent training. Dogs have not been adequately taught what is expected of them.

Rather than using the dominance model to explain the overall situation, it is far better to tackle each problem as an individual event. By teaching dogs each task with positive reinforcement, it will not only allow dogs to learn what is expected effectively but will also strengthen the relationship with the owner.

By developing the relationship in positive ways, you become the most important thing in your dog's life, which in turn increases obedience and makes training easier.

Other behaviour routinely cited as dominant include:

- ❖ Jumping up
- ❖ Attention seeking
- ❖ Begging

These types of problems are far more likely to be the result of actions that have been rewarded by the owner in the past.

Aggression

Dog aggression is routinely misinterpreted as dominance.

The most common incidents of aggression are associated with fear. If this is treated with the view that the dog is challenging the owner's authority, often it will be treated with aversive methods, driving fear and compounding the problem.

Growling and/or showing teeth is a way for your dog to let you know that it is not coping with a situation. By this time, many other body language cues have been missed, and the dog has had to resort to stronger indications.

Dogs should never be punished for growling. This is a normal part of canine communication and a clear warning that if pressed, a bite may follow.

If dogs become afraid to growl because they have been punished for it in the past, we end up with a potentially dangerous situation. A dog will bypass these strong warning signals and go straight for the bite.

If your dog is showing aggressive behaviour it is important that you consult a qualified behaviourist, rather than a dog trainer, as this is a specialised area.

The sooner the situation is assessed the more likely it is to get a positive outcome.

A full detailed history should be taken to diagnose the problem accurately so that correct treatment can be applied.

Dogs Social Behaviour

Dogs are not pack animals.

It is true to say that dogs are social by nature and will usually prefer company to isolation. When dogs live together in multi dog households do they form a strict hierarchical society as defined by pack rule theory? Do groups of dogs have defined dominant, subordinate and submissive members?

Having shared the last 20 years of my life living with a 'pack' of dogs (I lived with nine dogs for many years) and closely observing canine social interactions, I can safely say that the answer is no. Like human beings, dogs have individual personalities and individual dogs value different resources. Take as an example the social behaviour of my dogs at the present time:

Storm (Husky) will be assertive with the other dogs where toys are concerned, this is his favourite resource. If he notices any of the other dogs playing with a toy he will take it off them, take it to his toy 'stash' and defend it in order to prevent the other

- -

dogs gaining access. On his terms he will invite the other dogs to share his toys if he decides he wants a game of tug of war, however he is always delighted if the humans want to engage with his toys and will give them up on command without any problem.

Buddy (Greyhound x) will assert himself in competition for human attention and physical contact, this is the resource he values the most. He will barge everyone else out of the way to get attention and when he sees the brush coming out for grooming - he insists on being first in the queue.

Charlie (Shih Tzu) is food orientated and will steal food off other members of the group and defend his food in no uncertain terms. None of my other dogs will challenge him in this situation.

Suzie (Shih Tzu) doesn't value any particular resource. She will however tell Storm off in no uncertain terms if he is overly rough during play and he will submit to her.

Bilbo (Shih Tzu terrier x) is 15 years old and really appreciates a bit of comfort. If Suzie is taking up the only available space on the couch, he will sit on top of her until she gives up and gets off. Bilbo will however get off the couch on command without any problem.

They will all take it in turns to instigate play and social interactions and they will all, at one time or another, show either assertive or submissive behaviour to each other depending on the specific circumstance.

The notion that dogs have a linear hierarchical social system i.e. alpha dominates all, beta dominates omega and omega must submit to everyone else, is not apparent at all.

RANK REDUCTION – THE TRUTH

People who work along the lines of pack rule theory believe that problems are caused by dominance. With this view they may recommend using rank reduction techniques to rectify training and behavioural problems.

According to the theory, this is supposed to communicate to the dog that the owner is 'boss' and the dog is the subordinate. This usually consists of a total lifestyle change for the dog and a detrimental change in the relationship between owner and their pet.

Outlined below are the theoretical pack rules and their corresponding rank reduction techniques, along with comments regarding the affect that these changes may have.

Alphas eat first and are entitled to the best food

Technique 1 – Change the feeding regime so that the dog has to wait until the humans have eaten before they are allowed any food.

Withholding an expected reward i.e. denying your dog his food at the usual time, constitutes punishment. Dogs will not understand any other significance to this change in feeding regime in the beginning.

Dogs will soon adapt however, and the later feeding time will soon become the norm for the dog. This has no hierarchical implications.

Technique 2 – The owner must stand in front of the dog and eat a biscuit or similar, so that the dog witnesses the owner eating before being given their own food.

This consistent behaviour by the owner, will just become a clear signal that the dog's dinner is imminent – nothing more.

As discussed earlier, when food is scarce wolves will feed lactating females and pups first. Concerning domestic dogs, food is a resource which some may value more than others. The order of feeding does not have any connection with dominance or alpha status.

Alphas are entitled to the most elevated and comfortable resting places

Technique 1 – Dogs must never be allowed access to your lap or the couch, bed or bedroom under any circumstances. Access to upstairs should also be denied.

If dogs are used to this type of access and physical contact and the rules suddenly alter, it is a confusing lifestyle change, constituting punishment that can increase stress, anxiety and could possibly result in aggressive confrontation. This also affects negative changes in the nature of the relationship between the owner and the dog.

Technique 2 – The owner must stand in the dogs bed to show him that she/he is entitled to all resting places including the dogs own bed.

It is not clear what this will achieve from the dog's perspective, certainly there will be no recognition of authoritarian expression.

Wolves in the wild will often seek a high vantage point - this is not exclusive to breeding animals, in fact several members of the pack will share elevated positions and take it in turn to occupy the high ground as lookout. This has no connection to dominance or social status.

Alphas must not be disturbed when resting

Technique – If your dog is asleep on the floor and you want to move past them, instead of stepping around them, wake them up and make them move out of your way, to show them your status is higher.

From the dog's point of view they have been woken up, made to move for no apparent reason, followed by the owner walking away. This has no association with dominance and can damage relationships.

There is no evidence to support this rule applies to wolves, or dogs.

Alphas instigate all social interactions without exception

Technique – Dogs must be completely ignored if they are looking for any type of attention, fuss or games. All social interactions are to be instigated by the owner which should only occur when the dog is not asking.

This type of change in the owner's behaviour damages relationships.

This rule has no foundation in reality. Both wolves in the wild and domestic dogs living together, will take it in turns to instigate social interactions – this has no bearing on social status.

Alphas lead the pack from the front to make sure the environment is safe

Technique – The dog must always walk either beside you or behind you, and should never be allowed go through any doorway in front of you.

Both of these techniques are almost impossible to implement with any consistency.

There is no evidence of this behaviour in wolves. When travelling, wolves are not always led by the breeding pair. As discussed earlier often younger and faster pack members lead the hunt, with the more experienced and larger members coming in at the end for the kill.

- -

The Alpha Role

The alpha role is utilised when it is believed that a dog is getting ideas above its station. This is supposed to put a dog in its place.

Technique – The dog is forced to the floor on its back, and pinned by the throat.

Dogs will not associate this with authority. They will learn that humans are unpredictable and dangerous,which will result in fear and loss of trust. This is fundamentally damaging to the relationship between owner and dog, and can lead to many more serious behavioural problems associated with stress and anxiety and could lead to fear aggression.

Neither wolves nor dogs ever behave in this way towards each other. They will offer submissive body language as an appeasement to defuse a situation; they will never force another animal into this position.

[1]

---

[1]Further reading on Dominance and Pack Rule Theory-
http://www.dogtrainingkerry.com/dominance.html

IN CONCLUSION

If dogs do not display these types of imaginary rules in the course of their natural social behaviour, how are we to expect that they will recognise the significance of those rules when applied by us?

In my own house, despite the fact that several of the 'pack rules' are broken on a daily basis, we do not experience any dominance issues or training problems; my dogs are all confident, happy and obedient. They have been taught the rules of acceptable behaviour with consistency and positive reinforcement and consequently have formed a strong bond with us - their human companions.

90% of dog training is down to the good relationship you have with your dog. When it is based on consistency, reward, mutual respect and trust – training is easy.

Applying pack rule theory seriously damages the bond between owner and dog. This theory states that we have to show our dogs 'who is boss' and take the Alpha position for them to respect and obey us.

Suggesting that problems occur because our dogs are trying to assert their authority over us, causes the development of a negative and detrimental approach. Dogs become less like companions and more like a threat.

Do we really want a relationship with our pets on this basis?

HOUSE RULES

Forget about pack rules.

Only you can decide what is and what isn't acceptable where your own dog is concerned.

It is important to sit down with all family members to decide what house rules are applicable to your dog.

What areas of the house is your dog allowed access to?

Is your dog allowed on the couch, access to the bedrooms or the bed?

The most important thing is to decide what the rules are - and stick to them.

Everyone in the household must respect and uphold the house rules - be consistent. If some of the family are encouraging your dog to get up on the bed and others are telling them off for the same behaviour, it causes confusion which can lead to stress, hyperactivity and possibly even aggression.

Dogs on the Couch

Many individuals using the pack rule model will tell you that you must never allow dogs on the couch or the bed, as this will indicate that your dog's status is higher than yours which will lead to dominance issues with your dog.

As discussed previously this is not the case. What is the point of having a lap dog, if you have to deny them access to your lap?

If you enjoy cuddling up with your dog on the couch or the bed, that is entirely up to you. They are part of your house rules and your decision. However, to avoid potential problems, dogs that have access to the couch and/or the bed should be taught some basic rules:-

Access by invitation

If dogs are allowed to jump on the couch whenever they feel like it, this might not only be inconvenient for you but may not be appreciated by your visitors. Not everyone loves your dog as much as you do.

It is important therefore to teach dogs clear commands or visual cues, for both 'up' and 'off'. This can be achieved by using the same positive training methods outlined in the following chapters and should be practised during your training sessions.

Have a comfortable alternative

Make sure that your dog has a comfortable bed of their own as an alternative. Teach them to go onto their bed on command. You can use this when it is not convenient for them to be on the couch or bed.

Avoid sending them to their own bed in a negative fashion or as punishment, always as a positive alternative.

SECTION 3

THE 'NUTS AND BOLTS' OF TRAINING

Normal Dog Behaviour

Intelligence

How Dog's Learn

What Constitutes a Reward?

Primary Reinforcers

Rewards Based on Social Behaviour

Self Rewarding Behaviour

Training Techniques

Suitable Environments for Learning

The Importance of Timing

Markers – What they are and how to use them

Clicker Training

Verbal Marker

Phasing Out and Intermittent Rewards

Introducing and Using Commands

Using Hand Signals and Visual Cues

THE DOG'S MIND

In this section we are going to look at normal canine behaviour, basic principles of how dogs learn, what dogs find rewarding as well as dismantling the 'nuts and bolts' of positive reinforcement training.

Learning these basic elements will give you a deeper understanding of how and why positive reinforcement gains the best and most reliable results. Exploring these aspects is fundamental for successful training and gaining an insight into behaviour drives and problem solving.

What is Normal Dog Behaviour?

Dogs are predators and although hunting for food is not generally necessary for domestic pets, dogs' brains are still programmed for this behaviour. Normal predatory behaviour consists of scent- sight- stalk- chase- kill.

Other natural behaviours include barking, chewing, digging, foraging and defending members of their social group and territory.

These instincts, to greater or lesser degrees are hard wired into dogs and need to be expressed. It is important therefore to allow our dogs to explore these natural behaviours in positive ways.

Over generations of selective breeding we have genetically engineered different breeds to perform specific working tasks. Depending on the type of activity required we have retained, strengthened or diluted different aspects of these instinctive behaviours and in some cases manipulated the intensity of the senses.

For example, dogs that have been bred for herding such as sheepdogs and collies, have increased stalk behaviour and a strong impulse to chase, but a vastly diluted kill instinct. We want them to herd and 'chase' livestock with causing harm or injury. Some herding breeds were also bred to protect livestock, such as the Komodor and the Great Pyrenees, so these breeds will also display strong protective and guarding tendencies.

Hunting hounds and terriers were bred to assist us in hunting game, other predators and vermin control, so have retained all predatory behaviour including a strong prey drive. Short legged terriers were bred to dig out prey, so tend to be prolific hobby diggers. Sight hounds such as Greyhounds are bred for speed to capture fast agile prey, have keen vision and motion detection, where as scent hounds such as Bloodhounds and Beagles have been bred with increased scenting ability and stamina, for tracking over long distances.

If you have a working breed as a companion, it is helpful to consider their original purpose in order to not only understand the way they behave, but to channel their 'talents' into something positive. This obviously applies to all dogs, not just recognised working breeds; a good indication of a dog's strongest instincts usually reflects in the type of activities they enjoy.

If we do not allow them to use their natural behaviour in a positive way, they are likely to express them in ways that may not be acceptable to us.

Intelligence

Some years ago, staff at Battersea Dogs Home were baffled when each morning they arrived to find many of the kennel doors wide open with a number of dogs loose, food from the kitchens spread all over the floors and the place in general chaos.

There were no signs of any break-in; they just couldn't figure out what was going on. Whispers of ghostly activity and poltergeists began to circulate as the explanation for such strange events. It was odd that it was always the same collection of dogs that were loose each morning.

After a couple of weeks of the same ongoing activity, they decided to install CCTV cameras to find out just what was going on overnight.

It turned out to be 'Red' a Lurcher, who had worked out with persistent effort using his nose, tongue and teeth he could undo the bolt on the outside of his kennel door.

After helping himself to the best food from the kitchen, he proceeded down the block unbolting other kennel doors and letting out all of his mates. The rest of the night was spent in a free for all play session and an all you can eat buffet from the kitchen.

This demonstrates impressive problem solving skills, bearing in mind the bolt was on the outside of the kennel door. Red also displayed a high level of intelligence by only pursuing these activities when all the humans had left the building, making sure he got the best food before choosing to let out the dogs he particularly liked to socialise with.

Staff put an end to Red's nocturnal activities by fitting a strong padlock to his kennel door. Red continued to try and work around this problem without success, until he found his forever home shortly after.

Dogs are intelligent, extremely adaptive and have some impressive problem solving skills.

Their capacity to learn makes training them easy, but this can also work against us.

If we do not channel this intelligence in positive ways, they will engage their brains in ways that we usually do not appreciate. Bored dogs get up to all sorts of mischief.

You will find lots of information on stimulating your dog's mind in Section 5.

How Dogs Learn

In simple terms the basic principle of how dogs learn: If they exhibit a behaviour that elicits a reward, they are more likely to repeat it.

For instance if your dog sits and the action is reinforced with a reward, the behaviour is more likely to occur. The more frequently it is repeated and rewarded – the stronger it becomes.

If they exhibit a behaviour that is not rewarding, it is less likely to occur.

For instance if your dog jumps up and you completely ignore them, your dog will learn that jumping up is an unrewarding action and the behaviour will get weaker and less likely to occur.

What Constitutes a Reward?

What do dogs find rewarding?

Like humans, each dog will find different things and experiences rewarding.

In order to teach your dog in a positive way you need to establish what she/he values and is willing to work for. This can then be used as a reinforcer (reward) for desirable behaviour.

Generally the most effective rewards are primary reinforcers.

Primary Reinforcers

A primary reinforcer is something that satisfies a biological need.

Food is one of the strongest reinforcers for behaviour, most dogs will work well for food or treats.

You could also say that rewards based on instinctive behaviour fulfil a biological need. For dogs with a strong chase instinct a retrieval game would be a good reinforcer, and dogs with a stronger prey drive would value a tug of war game, or squeaky (kill) toy as a reward.

Rewards based on social behaviours

Dogs are social animals; they need company and enjoy attention and physical contact.

Giving attention at the wrong time can inadvertently contribute to undesirable behaviour. This is particularly the case if there has been a lack of, or insufficient positive reinforcement training. Often owners experience problem behaviour because they have attempted to stop behaviour by trying to teach the dog that it is wrong.

If your dog is presenting problem behaviour that you have tried to correct and the behaviour is not improving or indeed getting worse, your dog is finding your response rewarding in some way.

For example:- Dog jumps up and the owner may respond by: -

- ❖ Looking/eye contact = reward
- ❖ Speaking = reward
- ❖ Shouting = reward that increases excitement
- ❖ Pushing the dog away = rewarding game that increases excitement

In fact, any response by you to behaviour – can be a potential reward to your dog.

Dogs learn the best way to gain your attention is to behave in a way that elicits your best responses.

Unfortunately we inadvertently reinforce undesirable behaviour by trying to teach the dog that it is wrong.

Consequently the best way to work with dogs is to respond and reward good behaviour – teach them what is right - not attempt to actively teach them what is wrong.

Self-rewarding Behaviour

Some dog behaviours both natural and learned can be self-rewarding. These types of behaviours if left unchecked or undirected can become stronger.

Examples of natural self-rewarding behaviours:

Chasing – The dog chases a cat, bird, person on a bike, the object of the chase 'runs' away. Both the act of chasing and the result is rewarding.

Guarding and barking – The postman comes to the door, the dog barks, the postman leaves. Barking is rewarding and the retreat of the postman reinforces the behaviour.

Examples of learned self-rewarding behaviour

Bin Raiding – The dog gets access to the rubbish and finds something nice to eat. The behaviour has been reinforced and worth repeating.

Counter Surfing – If the dog has managed to steal food left out on the kitchen counter, the action has been reinforced and worth repeating.

Information on how to deal with these types of issues can be found in later sections.

Summary

If your dog is rewarded for an action, the behaviour will become stronger and more likely to occur.

If your dog presents a behaviour that is not rewarding, it will weaken and be less likely to occur.

A reward is whatever your dog values.

Any reaction by you (positive or negative), can potentially reinforce and strengthen behaviour.

Always teach what is right – not what is wrong.

Some dog behaviours both natural and learned can be self rewarding.

TRAINING TECHNIQUES

In this chapter we are going to look at suitable environments for learning, the mechanics of positive reinforcement training using markers and how to gradually phase out continuous rewards.

Suitable Environments for Learning

When trying to teach something new it is important that the environment is free from distractions.

Dogs cannot focus on learning if they are surrounded with stimulating sights, sounds and smells. Begin by training indoors or in an enclosed space away from distractions. This makes it easier to focus your dog's attention.

Keep training sessions short, 10-20 minutes is usually enough for most dogs. If your training has been going well and then your dog begins to be unresponsive, you have probably over-worked them or concentrated on the same task for too long If this occurs, try and ask for an easy action so you can reward them and end the session on a positive note. Keep training sessions short and varied.

If you have more than one dog, begin training on an individual basis Dogs cannot focus on learning if they are distracting each other. When each dog has an understanding of what you are trying to teach, you can then begin to work them together.

Avoid training if you are tired or stressed, you will lack patience and your dog will pick up on your emotions, which may affect their ability to learn.

Progressing to more Stimulating Environments

If you only practise training in the house, your dog will only respond to the commands in that situation. Once she/he has learnt a command and is responding reliably indoors, you can begin to increase the environmental stimulation in gradual stages.

Start by practising in the garden, which has slightly more distractions but is still familiar territory. Once you are getting reliable results in the garden, progress to practising when you are out walking in quiet locations. The environment is more interesting and has slightly more distractions.

Avoid giving commands if there is too much going on nearby or if your dog is in a heightened state - this will only set you up for failure. You must be able to focus your dog's attention, thereby giving your dog the best opportunity to gain success and reward. This will result in more reliable training, improve focus and help to build confidence. Success breeds success.

You can gradually build up to more stimulating and distracting environments, until eventually, you should be able to keep your dog's focus no matter what is going on around you.

Practising your Training

If you don't use it, you lose it!

You do not necessarily need to set time aside every day to practise your training, just incorporate it into the course of everyday life. Ask your dog to do something obedient before giving any type of reward. For instance when feeding, putting on the lead for walks or while playing games.

The Importance of Timing

Dogs live in the moment. Therefore your reaction time for reinforcement is crucial in order to indicate clearly what action, or behaviour is desired. Even a few seconds delay in response may prevent your dog from associating the reward with the action.

This is why it is important to have a consistent method of instant response such as a marker when teaching new behaviour. This is covered in detail in the following sections.

The relevance of timing is also worth mentioning here in relation to punishment. As with positive reinforcement, if you punish your dog after the event there is no association between the punishment and the action.

A scenario that I frequently encounter:

From the owner's perspective –

Owner returns home to find that their dog has damaged something of value. The owner is angry and convinced that the dog knows what it has done

- -

wrong because they look 'sheepish' which is interpreted as guilt. They may shout or physically punish the dog for the behaviour.

What usually happens at this point is the destructive behaviour becomes worse and more frequent; the owner increases the punishment accordingly as they believe the dog is acting out of spite.

From the dog's perspective –

The dog has been left alone for too long with nothing positive to occupy them; they get bored and look for something to pass the time and find something that is easily accessible to play with. Some time later the owner returns and as soon as they enter the house, they behave in a very aggressive manner.

The dog does not associate the owner's behaviour as a consequence of something that occurred in the past, but in response to the owner's obvious anger they will offer submissive body language. When dogs offer this type of appeasement to another dog, it usually diffuses aggression. Instead of the expected reduction of aggression, the owner gets even more angry, as they see the appeasement display as an admittance of guilt. The reaction of the owner causes confusion and stress.

Consequently the next time the owner leaves the house, the dog becomes anxious because they associate the return of the owner with unpredictable and frightening results.

The build up of stress and anxiety in anticipation of their return, drives destructive behaviour and often other problems associated with stress and a cycle of increased destruction and punishment ensues.

The original problem was caused by boredom and lack of positive activities, the continued and escalating destruction is a result of inappropriate punishment.

The fault for the original problem lies with the owner for not supplying toys and positive activities and leaving items of value in easy reach.

Ideas for home alone activities, mental stimulation and environmental interest are covered in detail in Section 5.

Markers– What They Are and How to Use Them

A marker is usually an audible sound that can be delivered as a first and rapid response to a desired action, which gives a clear and consistent signal to your dog that what they are doing, or what they have just done, is right.

Markers are used in conjunction with a reinforcer (reward) such as food, games or toys.

This method utilises Classical Conditioning, which is the pairing of two unrelated stimuli so that an association is formed between the two.

The dog hears the marker, which is quickly followed by the reward (treat, toy or game). It is amazing how fast dogs build an association between the 'mark' and the reward. The 'mark' soon becomes a reinforcer in itself because of the association with the reward. This system is a fast and effective way of teaching new behaviour.

There are two systems that 'mark' behaviour - clicker training or verbal markers. Choose the method that suits you best.

Clicker Training

A clicker is a small mechanical device that makes a distinctive 'click' sound when pressed, The 'click' should be activated the instant your dog offers the desired action. This is immediately followed by the reinforcer – 'click' and reward (treat, toy or game)

The advantages of using clicker training:-

❖ It is a unique sound that your dog wouldn't hear in any other circumstance and therefore becomes a powerful and distinct marker for desirable behaviour.

❖ The clicker is a more consistent marker as it always sounds the same, no matter who is working the dog.

❖ A good tool for problem solving, shaping and reshaping undesirable behaviour.

❖ It is a calm marker delivered without emotion preventing overexcited responses.

Possible disadvantages of using clicker training:-

- ❖ Clickers are small and can be difficult to use for people who suffer medical conditions such as arthritis.

- ❖ Sometimes you just don't have enough hands! If you are training when out walking, it can be difficult to manage the lead, treats or toys and the clicker.

- ❖ Clickers can be misplaced or lost.

Verbal Markers

If you choose a verbal marker as your first response keep it simple, calm and consistent.

For example you could choose 'Good' or 'Yes'. The verbal marker should be immediately followed by the reinforcer – 'Yes' and reward (treat, toy or game) or 'Good' and reward (treat, toy or game)

The advantages of verbal reinforcement:-

- ❖ You are always equipped to mark behaviour.
- ❖ Hands free marking.

The disadvantages of verbal markers:-

- ❖ Not as consistent with different handlers.
- ❖ Some dogs may overreact to verbal markers if delivered with too much emotion.

Phasing Out and Intermittent Rewards

When teaching new behaviour use continuous reinforcement i.e. mark and reward your dog every time she/he gets it right. This is the best method to ensure that a new response quickly becomes a well established behaviour.

Once the behaviour is well established and reliable, you should gradually reward the performance of that action less and less often.

This should be done in a gradual fashion. In fact, it should be done so slowly that your dog will not even realise that he is being weaned from a continuous reward.

One method of achieving this is to move the goal posts. Instead of rewarding each action individually, you can begin to string multiple commands together. Start with two commands such as 'sit' and 'down'. Mark and reward at the end of the sequence. Then add a third (varying the commands and the order) for instance 'down' and 'sit' and 'touch', mark and reward at the end of the sequence, and so on.

You should randomly reward a reasonable percentage of each established command once your dog is past the learning stage. This is referred to as an intermittent reward, which is a random reward in response to repeated behaviour.

Not knowing when the action will receive a reward creates incentive and enthusiasm. Choose their best and quickest responses to reinforce and your dog will work harder in an effort to achieve the reward. Your dog's responses should become quicker, stronger and more reliable.

By stringing together commands in different orders, you will naturally give random rewards for different commands depending what the last command in the sequence is. Having said that, vary your approach to really keep your dog on his toes. Be unpredictable in the amount of responses the dog has to give each time, occasionally just ask for one response, sometimes two, three or four etc.

Replace treats with their usual food.

Take out a portion of food your dog would usually get in his bowl and use it to reinforce good behaviour. In this way, your dog has to earn his food, which is much more stimulating than getting it for free in a dish.

Continue to intermittently reward with treats on the best and fastest responses or when you are teaching something new.

If at some point your dog stops responding to a particular command, go back and concentrate on that individual action using constant rewards until reliable.

Force Free Training

Dogs will instinctively resist applied physical pressure. The more force that is applied, the more they will resist.

Try placing your hand on your dog's side and begin to apply a little pressure as if to push him away.

- -

You will find that he will resist the pressure and push against your hand. Any increase in pressure will be matched by his resistance to it. This principal of force resistance is often a factor when dogs pull on the lead.

When the lead is taut, pressure is applied to the front of the throat (collar) or chest (harness), driving the dog to push against the pressure and pull harder.

Often owners try to remedy this by using a choke chain which makes the problem worse. This usually results in the owner getting dragged down the road while the dog chokes, the tightened chain causing damage to the trachea and causing pain and discomfort. Not only does this cause physical pain, but also stress and anxiety, which can also cause hyperactivity which further aggravates the problem.

You will find instructions on how to teach loose lead walking in the following sections.

If you try and force your dog into a position, (forcing their back end down into a sit for example) you will notice that as soon as pressure is applied, your dog will stiffen their legs and you will have to apply quite a lot of pressure to force your dog into a sitting position. In this case your dog isn't learning to sit, rather they are learning to resist sitting.

It is much more effective to use hands off training. This is where you ask your dog to think and make choices and reward them for making the right choice. With this approach you are stimulating their mind as well as shaping their behaviour. This method facilitates fast learning and reliable training.

Force free training can be achieved by rewarding a naturally occurring behaviour, using a treat or toy as a lure or using your body language to encourage.

You will find step by step instructions on the various techniques for hands off training in Section 4.

'Mark' refers to your chosen method: Use either a clicker or a verbal marker such as 'Good' or 'Yes'. Reward refers to the option that best suits your dog: Treat, game or toy.

Make sure the reward follows in quick succession to the mark

Summary

When teaching something new, pick an environment that is free from distractions

Increase environmental distractions gradually as training becomes established

Keep training sessions reasonably short and varied

Timing is important to correctly associate a reward with an action

Marking behaviour with either a clicker or a verbal marker, gives a clear signal that what they are doing, or what they have just done is right

Phase out rewards by moving the goal posts and giving intermittent rewards

Forcing your dog into a position teaches resistance

Hands off, force free methods, facilitates fast learning and reliable training

INTRODUCING AND USING COMMANDS

In this chapter we are going to look at the way commands should be introduced and how to use them correctly.

This is an area where owners often go wrong, causing confusion that can affect the reliability of training.

Do not introduce a verbal command until your dog has learnt the behaviour

One of the most common mistakes when teaching dogs something new is to use a command before the dog has learnt what the command means. Dogs do not understand English.

If you introduce a command too early, it is just a sound that keeps coming out of your mouth that has no association with any particular action.

They do understand which behaviour elicits a reward; if an action is reinforced they are more likely to repeat it. The more times they repeat the behaviour and are rewarded, the stronger the behaviour becomes.

When trying to teach something new, either use hands off training to encourage the desired action or reward behaviour your dog presents naturally.

When you have achieved a few successes, you can then begin to associate a command for the action. This will be covered in detail in Section 4.

Only use simple verbal commands and keep the volume down

You do not need to shout at your dog to get your point across, in fact the quieter the commands – the better.

Tone of voice is everything; shouting commands can confuse your dog and cause stress. When dogs are anxious they cannot focus or think clearly which inhibits learning. Louder does not equal clearer.

It is comparable to visiting a foreign speaking country and thinking that shouting will make you more understandable.

Keep to simple one word commands and resist the temptation to add in your dog's name. For instance when asking for a sit, just say 'sit', not 'sit down' 'Rex sit' 'Sit Rex' or various other combinations.

Remember dogs do not understand words, they learn to associate a particular sound with a particular action. So keep it simple and consistent.

Once you have established a verbal command – Only give it once

You will not achieve reliable training by repeating commands over and over. Often owners not only repeat, but also raise the volume as they go along, sit, sit, sit, SIT, SIT until eventually they sit. The dog is then rewarded for sitting.

This becomes an optional request, it encourages slow responses as the dog learns that if she/he finally gets around to it, she/he will be rewarded all the same.

It can be confusing for your dog. Repeating yourself is not consistent and does not sound the same. You are not only varying the amount of times you repeat, but the spacing between repeats is often different.

Remember, dogs do not understand language; they associate a particular sound, with a particular action.

Successful dog training involves patience- Play the waiting game

Once you have successfully introduced a command, say it once and then just wait.

Allow your dog time to think about what she/he has learned and give them time to comply. During this waiting time keep eye contact but resist the temptation to repeat yourself. You must give your dog time to process this new information. This can take some time to begin with, you must be patient.

If you have given your dog a reasonable amount of time to comply and it was unsuccessful, turn away and ignore them for a few seconds before starting a fresh attempt.

This teaches that compliance elicits a reward, non compliance results in no reward/lack of attention.

This is using two aspects of Operant Conditioning, where an association is made between a behaviour and a consequence:-

Positive reinforcement - when a behaviour (sit) is followed by a stimulus (treat) results in an increase in the frequency of the behaviour.

Negative punishment - when a behaviour (failure to sit) is followed by the removal of a stimulus (lack of reward and removal of attention) leads to a decrease in behaviour.

Using Hand Signals or Visual Cues

There are advantages to using hand signals or visual cues in conjunction with, instead of or as well as verbal commands.

Dogs are capable of learning more than one cue (both verbal and visual) for the same behaviour. For instance for the action stay, you could use a verbal command 'stay' and/or a palm forward flat hand signal.

Dogs are tuned in to body language as this is their main means of communication.

You will notice that sometimes your dog seems to read your mind and will start to get excited when you have decided to take them out, even before you have begun to put on your shoes or coat. You give off subtle body language signals that your dog picks up on.

If you use hand signals or arm movements as a cue for specific behaviour make sure you always use the same hand or arm, otherwise your signals are inconsistent and confusing.

Many years ago I rescued a deaf Cavalier King Charles Spaniel; the owners were having difficulties coping with his disability and were considering putting him to sleep.

I trained Radar using sign language. As our means of communication was purely visual, he constantly 'checked in', the slightest movement grabbing his attention.

Using visual cues encourages your dog to 'check in' more frequently, which improves focus and gives you more control.

Dogs that suffer hearing decline in later life are still able to respond reliably to training.

Summary

Do not introduce a verbal command until you have achieved a few successful repeats of the behaviour.

Softly, softly, catchy monkey - Keep commands quiet.

If you are using a verbal command – Keep it simple.

Only give your command once – then just wait. Give your dog time to process new information and think about what they have learned.

Dogs are capable of learning more than one cue for an action.

- -

SECTION 4

LET'S GET TRAINING!

STEP BY STEP INSTRUCTIONS

Toileting on Command

Teaching Touch

Teaching Sit

Teaching Down

Teaching Drop

Teaching Loose Lead Walking

Recall Training

TEACHING THE BASICS

In this section you will find step by step instructions outlining various positive reinforcement methods to teach basic commands.

There is usually more than one way of teaching an action, so choose the method that best suits you and your dog.

If your dog is not responding, try an alternative method until you find the one that works.

Keep training sessions short and varied.

TOILETING ON COMMAND

When house training puppies or older dogs, take them outside at regular intervals. Actively teaching your dog a specific command associated with going to the toilet, helps increase the possibility of house training success as you can begin to get your dog to 'empty' on cue.

This is particularly useful before allowing them access to the rest of the house, before settling them down for bed or before leaving them unattended during the day.

Make sure you are equipped with your reinforcer (treats or toys) and your clicker if you are using one.

When you take your dog out, stay with them but resist the temptation to interact with them as you really want them to focus on with the job in hand.

You will need patience as it can take some time before anything is produced.

Have your clicker ready in one hand if you are using one and have the reward in the other. As soon as they squat get ready, when they have finished, mark immediately with either your clicker or your verbal marker and follow quickly with the reward. You do not have to say anything at this stage, all we want to do is reward the behaviour we want to encourage.

If you are working with a puppy, stay outside for a bit longer as sometimes they will urinate two or three times in short succession.

Each time they are successful, mark and reward. Stick to this regime for a couple of garden sessions before attempting to introduce a command for the action.

Introduce the Command

The next stage is to decide what command or cue you want to use.

Some people use 'busy' or 'potty', it doesn't matter what it is, but pick something simple. Decide on a verbal cue for the behaviour and stick to it.

We want to form an association between the sound or your command and the action of going to the toilet. This is achieved by introducing the command while they are still in the process. So as soon as they squat say your cue and once they finish,

- -

mark and reward. Keep to this stage for a few outdoor sessions.

The next stage is to take them outside and give the command just before they squat. Watch for the body language, you should be picking up the signals at this stage, when you see the early warning signs say your cue before your dog begins.

Mark and reward when they have completed the action.

After a few repeats at this stage your dog should be associating the sound of the cue, with the action of going to the toilet. You can now begin to give your command as soon as you take them out. Only say it once, be patient and resist the temptation to repeat the command, give your dog time to process the information. As soon as they squat, mark and reward the behaviour. You should find that their response times improve with each success.

After a few days, your dog should be eliminating on command.

TEACHING TOUCH

Teaching this action has many advantages and is a good place to begin basic training.

The aim of the touch command is to train your dog to touch your hand with their nose.

It is a good technique to improve focus and by changing the position of your hand, you can utilise it to teach other commands such as sit, down and heel.

Once established you can work further and further away from your dog, giving you an effective method of moving your dog around without force and laying down a good foundation for recall training.

It is also a good counterproductive action for dogs that are inclined to 'mouth' or grab your hand with their teeth. This is a common problem with puppies and a good early command to teach.

Method for teaching the action 'touch'

Have the reward ready in one hand (if using a clicker, it should be in the same hand as the reward). This should be either tucked up by your chest, or behind your back. Place the other free hand palm forward, a few inches in front of your dog at nose level.

Dogs will nearly always investigate an offered hand by smelling it. Remember that your timing is crucial, so make sure you mark the behaviour the instant they make contact with their nose and follow it by giving the reward.

Be careful not to reward them if they make any contact with their teeth, this is not a behaviour that we want to encourage.

If your dog does not offer the behaviour, rub the scent of a treat on your hand and try again. Don't forget to be patient and allow some thinking time. Resist the temptation to move your hand to make contact with your dog's nose, always let them decide to take the action for themselves.

In this instance you have already introduced a visual cue; you will find quite quickly that when you put your hand down, your dog will offer you the behaviour.

You do not necessarily need to introduce a verbal command, but it is useful to have in place both verbal and visual cues.

How to introduce the 'touch' command

Once you have had a few successful repeats, you can introduce a 'touch' command. This should be done the instant your dog makes contact with your hand.

So the sequence is - offer your hand, as the dog makes contact say 'touch' followed quickly by the mark and reward.

When you have achieved a few successful repeats introducing a verbal command as the behaviour is offered, your dog should be associating the sound 'touch' with the action.

You can now try the command before they offer the behaviour – say 'touch' at the same time as offering your hand. Remember only say it once, then wait. Give your dog time to think about what she/he has learned.

Always mark and reward the behaviour when successful. If you have given your dog a good time to process the information and it has failed, turn away for a few seconds before trying again. This way you are beginning a new attempt, rather than repeating yourself.

Progressing the touch command

Practise getting your dog to touch both right and left hands. Only have one hand available, making sure the spare hand that holds the reward is tucked out of the way.

Once your dog is responding well, begin to work further away from your dog (in small stages) so your dog has to move toward you in order to successfully execute the behaviour. Practise at different distances from your dog. This should be built up over the course of a several training sessions.

If you are having difficulties, you might be trying to move too fast; so go back a stage.

At this point you can begin to move the goal posts by asking for more than one 'touch' before marking and rewarding the behaviour.

- -

Vary your approach so that for instance, you could ask for two touches on the right and one on the left hand before rewarding. The more you vary it the better.

If asking for consecutive touches on the same hand, the hand should be lifted to your chest in-between to give a clear indication that it is a new request, not repeating the command for an already successful action.

TEACHING SIT

There are several different methods to teach the action sit, choose the one that suits you best.

Method 1 – Natural

Wait until your dog sits of their own accord. The instant their backside touches the floor, mark the action and give the reward.

If she/he stays in position keep reinforcing the behaviour with the mark and reward. When your dog comes out of position, get another treat ready and wait.

As you have just rewarded your dog for sitting, you should find with a little patience, your dog will offer the behaviour again, mark and reward immediately.

The more you reinforce the behaviour, the more frequently it will be offered. Once you have had a few successful repeats move on to introducing the verbal command.

Method 2 – Lure and Reward

This method uses a treat to lure your dog into position.

Put a treat right on the end of your dog's nose and move it slightly to encourage your dog's head into a nose upward position keeping the treat right on the end of his nose, (if it is too high your dog may jump up) move the lure backward as if going

- -

between the eyes. You only need to move the treat an inch or two, trying to keep the lure in contact with the nose. Your dog should follow the treat and automatically go into a sit.

Mark the behaviour immediately and give the treat. Once you have had a few successful repeats move on to introducing your verbal command.

Method 3 – Utilising an established 'Touch'

If you have already taught your dog to 'touch', you can use your hand instead of a treat to lure into the sit position using the same process as Method 2.

Introduce the 'sit' command

Once you have had a few successful repeats, introduce the 'sit' command. This should be done as your dog is actively going into a sit.

So the sequence is – as your dog is actively going into the position say 'sit', mark and reward. Repeat the command three or four times as your dog is going into the sit, usually this is enough for them to begin to associate the sound 'sit' with the action of sitting.

You can now try using the command before the behaviour is offered. Remember, only say it once and wait. Give your dog time to process the information without interruption. Always mark and reward the behaviour when successful.

If you are not achieving the desired results, go back a stage.

Introduce your visual cue

Once you are getting a good response to the verbal command, decide what visual cue you want to use for sit.

The cue I use is to keep my right elbow against my body with my hand in a palm up position, raising the hand towards the right shoulder. You may choose something different; it doesn't matter providing your visual cue is consistent.

Give the visual cue at the same time as the 'sit' command. Mark and reward.

Repeat the visual cue three or four times in conjunction with the verbal command, then try dropping the verbal command and just try the visual cue. Keep the hand signal in position, give your dog time to think about what she/he has learned. Mark and reward if successful.

If you are not achieving the desired results, go back a stage.

Practise just using the 'sit' command, practise using the command in conjunction with the visual cue and practise your visual cue without the command. Your dog is quite capable of learning more than one cue for an action.

TEACHING DOWN

There are several different methods for teaching the action 'down'.

Method 1 – Natural

Wait until your dog lies down of his own accord, mark and reward immediately.

If she/he stays in the position keep rewarding. If they come out of position, get another treat ready and then just wait. As you have just rewarded your dog for the behaviour you will find with a little patience that the dog will offer the behaviour again; mark and reward.

The more often you reinforce the behaviour the more frequently it will be repeated.

When you have had a few successful repeats, move on to introducing the verbal command.

Method 2 – Lure and Reward with a treat

This method uses a treat to lure your dog into position.

Get your dog to sit. Crouch down facing your dog and place a treat right on the end of his nose. Slowly move the treat toward the floor going at your dog's pace. If you have moved too quickly and the treat looses contact with his nose, bring it back up and try again more slowly.

Don't forget to allow your dog room to get into the down position, you may have to move the treat slightly forward as you reach the floor to give your dog enough space; mark and reward if successful.

Keep using this method while you introduce your verbal command.

If you are having difficulty luring your dog with this method, try method 3.

Method 3 – Lure and Reward using your legs

Sit on the floor with your knees raised, leaving just enough space under your legs to allow your dog room to get underneath if lying down. Offer a treat under your legs and try and lure your dog through, moving the treat slowly to the other side. If they follow the treat they will have to lie down in order to fit; mark and reward if successful.

Some dogs will try and jump over the top. Just change hands and try and lure them through the other direction.

Keep using this method while you introduce your verbal command. Once your dog is beginning to form an association with the command 'down', progress to using Method 2 lure and reward in conjunction with your verbal command before trying to remove the use of the treat as a lure.

- -

Introduce the 'down' command

Once you have had a few successful repeats you can introduce the 'down' command (still using the lure) as the dog is actively going into the position.

So the sequence is - as your dog is in the process of going into position, say 'down', mark and reward.

Repeat the command three or four times as your dog is going into the down, usually this is enough for them to begin to associate the sound 'down' with the action of lying down.

The next stage is to remove the lure if you are using one.

Removing the Lure

Once your dog is responding to the command, you can begin to replace the lure with a visual cue.

Decide what visual cue you want to use for 'down'. Move the treat to the opposite hand. Move your signal hand to the floor using your chosen cue and give the command. Don't forget to say it once then wait.

If successful mark the behaviour, the reward should now be produced from the opposite hand.

If you are not achieving the desired results, go back a stage for a few repeats.

Progressing the visual cue

You can now begin to gradually move your hand signal higher and higher, until you are able to give the cue from a standing position.

This should to be done in gradual increments. Begin by stopping your hand an inch away from the floor while giving the command 'down'.

After a few repetitions, stop at 6 inches from the floor and so on. With practice you should be able to give the visual cue from a stand position.

This should be done over the course of several training sessions.

TEACHING DROP

There are two different methods for teaching the action 'drop'.

Method 1 – Using a toy and a treat

Play with your dog with a toy and encourage them to hold it in their mouth with lots of praise.

Put a treat on the end of their nose and watch as your dog considers his options. If he wants to take the treat, he must drop what is in his mouth. For some dogs this is a no-brainer, others will take a little time to commit to a decision. Be patient. As soon as the toy is released, mark immediately and reward with the treat.

After a few successful repeats you can introduce your verbal command.

Method 2 – Using two toys

You will need two similar toys, balls work really well for this method but any two toys your dog enjoys will suffice.

Give one of them to your dog, giving lots of praise and encouragement when he engages with it. When they are holding it in their jaws, start playing with the other toy. Make the toy in your hand more interesting than the one they have in their mouth.

Keep playing with the spare toy while your dog considers his options. Inevitably he will abandon the one he has, for the chance of a more interactive experience.

Mark immediately and reward by throwing the second toy. Retrieve the first toy and repeat.

After a few successes, introduce the verbal command.

Introduce the 'drop' command

Once you have had a few successful actions, introduce your command at the instant your dog drops the toy.

So the sequence is - as your dog is in the process of dropping the toy, give your chosen command, mark and reward.

Repeat the command three or four times as your dog is in the process of releasing the toy, usually this is enough for them to begin to associate the sound of the command with the action.

You can now try the command before they offer the behaviour – remember, only say it once, then wait. Give your dog time to think about what she/he has learned.

Always mark and reward the behaviour when successful.

If you are not achieving the desired results, go back a stage utilising the treat or the two toy method, in conjunction with the command.

Introduce the visual cue

Decide what visual cue you want to use for drop.

Give your visual cue at the same time as the 'drop' command. When you have achieved a few successful repeats, try the visual cue only. Keep your visual cue in position and give your dog time to think about what she/he has learned, mark and reward if successful.

If you are not achieving the desired results, go back to using the verbal command in conjunction with the visual cue.

LOOSE LEAD WALKING

If we do not teach dogs to walk properly on a loose lead, we cannot expect them not to pull.

As mentioned earlier dogs will resist applied pressure. The pressure that results on the front of the collar or harness from the action of pulling will encourage dogs to push against the pressure.

When teaching loose lead walking it is important that the handler doesn't apply tension to the lead. If your lead is in a straight rigid line, you need to relax your hands more. If you relax the lead your dog will stop resisting.

If you intend to show your dog it is best to have them work on your left. If not intending to show, it doesn't matter which side your dog works on.

If you are walking on a pavement, you want your dog on the inside away from the road. This could be either on your right or left depending on which direction you are walking. So it is useful to practise with your dog on both sides. Don't worry if they are not in a precise heel position, the most important thing is a relaxed, loose lead.

Equipment

There are a few alternatives for lead attachment, some safer than others.

Recommended -

For most dogs the body harness where the lead attaches in the middle of the back, is the safest and best option. Dogs usually accept these without any difficulty.

For extra strong dogs, a Halti head collar or similar, where the lead attaches under the chin. These are great tools if introduced correctly.

If you choose this option, you should spend a few days getting your dog used to it before you attempt to attach a lead.

The best method is to hold the nose band open with one hand and offer a treat in the middle of the opening. When your dog moves toward the treat, draw it through, so that s/he follows the treat voluntarily placing the band over the nose in the process. Give the treat straight away.

Do not attempt to do up the neck strap in the beginning and only keep the nose band in place for a few seconds. Give lots of praise, take it off, and repeat.

Gradually build up the time that the nose band is in place, making sure that you keep your dog distracted.

Once they are happy with this stage you can progress to doing up the neck strap, again for a few seconds to begin with, keeping your dog's focus with distractions.

Gradually build up the time that the collar is in place. If handled correctly, your dog should be quite happy to wear the head collar. At this stage you can attach a lead (preferably a light nylon lead, rather than a heavy chain lead) and begin lead training.

Not Recommended -

Choke chains tighten when the dog pulls, causing stress, breathing difficulties and damage to the throat and trachea. They teach dogs to pull more on the lead due to pressure resistance and cause injury and psychological damage.

Attaching a lead to a standard collar during training can be dangerous as sudden jerks to the neck can cause damage to the spine, particularly in developing dogs.

Where to begin Lead Training

It is much easier to begin lead training in a contained and limited environment.

The garden is the best place to start, as the environment is familiar and there are few distractions. If you attempt to teach loose lead work while out on a walk, your dog will not be able to concentrate on learning with all the environmental distractions.

Begin the training session in the garden by practising other already established commands. This way you are focusing attention and giving clear signals that this is a training/reward session.

After a few minutes, attach the lead while still continuing to practise your basic commands.

Circle Work using a Lure

When starting lead training it is better not to try and walk in a straight line.

Ask your dog to sit. Stand next to your dog with the lead handle in the hand on the opposite side from your dog. Make sure the length of your lead is adequate, so that when your arm is relaxed the lead is loose. Put a treat between your thumb and the palm of the hand nearest your dog and place the back of your hand to your dog's nose. She/he will smell the treat but won't be able to see it. Standing on one spot, try and get your dog to follow your hand as you turn in a circle. When you get round to your original starting position mark the behaviour, turn your hand and give the reward.

Once you have successfully repeated this, begin walking round in a small circle, still using your lure - mark and reward one rotation.

Practise on both sides and in both directions. If your dog is on your right hand side, you will be turning anti-clockwise, and if she/he is on your left, you will be rotating clockwise. Build up by gradually increasing the size of your circle.

Do not try and work at these exercises for too long, break up your lead training with other training and games.

Removing the Lure

Once your dog is responding well you can remove the lure. Put the treat in the opposite hand (the one holding the lead handle) and offer the back of your hand in the same way as you did when you had the treat in it. This will now become your visual cue. Mark and reward with the treat from the opposite hand.

Over the course of several training sessions, begin increasing the size of the circle and the amount of rotations your dog has to complete on a loose lead, before reinforcing the behaviour with the mark and reward.

Moving on to Circuits and Figure of Eights

The next stage is to expand your circle into an ellipse. You are now beginning to introduce straight lines into your circle work. It is useful to set up two objects to mark your circuit, anything that you may have handy, for instance a couple of buckets, plant pots or chairs.

Place them about 8-10 feet apart to begin with, but as you progress you can increase the distance between them.

Using your hand signal, and making sure that your lead is loose, get your dog to follow your hand around one object, down the straight line and stop at the second object, mark and reward.

Practise, gradually increasing the amount of circuits your dog has to complete before receiving the reward. If you are having difficulty, go back a stage. After a bit of practise you can begin to introduce figures of eights around your circuit markers.

Do not try and work at these exercises for too long, the level of concentration for both you and your dog is quite demanding, so break up your lead training with other training and games.

Begin Practising on Walks

Once your dog is getting the hang of walking on a loose lead in the garden you can begin to practise your training in other environments.

It is best to keep your short lead walks brief while under training.

Resist the temptation to walk too far in a straight line when out to begin with. Practise lots of direction changes and large ellipses just as you did in the garden. If at any time your dog pulls on the lead, stop, encourage them back and ask for a sit. Do a few circles before moving on.

Walking on a loose lead will soon become normal behaviour for your dog with perseverance and practise.

RECALL TRAINING

This is one of the most important and in my experience, one of the most frequently neglected commands. It is inadvisable to let your dog off the lead unless they recall on command reliably.

Unfortunately owners usually fail to recall their dogs successfully because:-

- ❖ The owner has no method of getting their dog's attention or focus.

- ❖ The dog has not been taught to come back on command.

- ❖ The dog is only called when there is trouble looming or their focus is on an approaching dog or some other stimulating situation - which results in failure.

- ❖ The owner shouts the dog's name, which is a familiar sound that has no association with any particular action.

Key points to teaching successful recall

Begin teaching recall in a familiar environment. This is not something that you should attempt to teach when out for a walk. There are far too many environmental distractions that inhibit your dog's ability to learn. So begin by teaching recall training in the house or garden.

Get your dog's attention

There is no point trying to recall your dog if it is not focused on you.

The most reliable method to achieve this is to use a dog whistle. My personal preference is an adjustable pitch dog whistle, rather than the silent type, as they have a nice strong audible tone that is pitched to grab your dog's attention. They are effective at cutting through the environment (even in high winds) and the sound carries much further than a human voice.

For recall I prefer to use the whistle instead of a verbal command; to begin with the whistle is used to get focus however it soon becomes the cue for the behaviour.

You may choose to introduce a verbal and or a visual cue, which can be achieved using the same methods as previously explained.

Invite them in using your body language

When you blow your whistle (a couple of short sharp blows) it should grab your dog's attention. As soon as your dog looks at you, reduce your body profile by either bending at the waste or crouching down. (Only reduce your profile as much as you need to in order to get the desired result). Be enthusiastic in your encouragement. This is a strong invitation for your dog to come to you and is generally successful.

When your dog approaches mark and reward the behaviour immediately. Practise for a few repetitions using your whistle and your body language to encourage them in. You should notice after a short time that your dog is beginning to move towards you as soon as she/he hears the whistle.

Although the whistle initially was used to get focus, it is now being associated with the recall action and becomes the command or cue for returning to you. Always mark and reward when successful.

Increase environmental distractions

Once you are achieving reliable results at home you can begin to practise recall when out for walks.

Do not let your dog off the lead until you have a reliable recall.

This is achieved by working your dog on an extendable lead. I prefer the extra long 26ft or 8m retractable lead.

WARNING - These leads should only be used in conjunction with a body harness, never attach a retractable lead to a collar or head collar for safety, sudden jerks on the neck can cause neck and spinal injuries. DO NOT allow your dog to take off at a full run on a retractable lead, by the time they get to the end, they have a lot of momentum. Only use the handle, never grab the lead as doing so may cause a burn injury.

Begin by practising in quiet locations. Resist the temptation to try a recall when there are too many distractions to begin with as this will result in failure. Recall your dog frequently, mark and reward and then release them again.

By doing this your dog is returning to you for a reward and then is regaining their freedom to explore the environment. It is important to practise recalling frequently during the course of every walk. This should be an ongoing activity.

While walking, do frequent and sudden direction changes. Turn back the way you just came or shoot off down a side path encouraging your dog to follow. If your dog learns that you are not always necessarily going to walk in a straight line and that you can be a little unpredictable, they will be more focused and aware of where you are. You will find quite quickly that as soon as you change direction, your dog will turn with you.

This is a good tool to have in place as a distraction technique if you see potential trouble looming. It interrupts your dog's focus before they can get into a heightened state and brings their attention back to you.

Increase environmental distractions as your dog's recall response progresses.

Summary

Keep training sessions short and varied.

Use whatever method that suits you and your dog best.

You can use different methods to teach different actions.

If you are failing to communicate what is required, try a different method.

Get your dog's attention before attempting to recall.

As your training becomes established begin practising in different environments.

SECTION 5

STIMULATING YOUR DOG'S MIND

Advantages of Mental Stimulation
Games

Self Rewarding Activities

Environmental Interest

Stimulating Walks

Training – Expand on the Basics

Sports and Activities

Advantages in the Twilight Years

- -

MENTAL STIMULATION AND GAMES

Quality Time and Building Bonds

In this section we are going to look at how to stimulate dogs with games, self rewarding activities and environmental interest.

These activities will result in a happy and fulfilled life for your dog and build a sound and enjoyable relationship with your companion.

Allowing dogs to partake and enjoy their natural behaviour and engage their brains in positive ways can prevent many behavioural problems.

Increasing mental stimulation has many benefits:-

- ❖ Reduces stress and anxiety
- ❖ Builds confidence
- ❖ Reduces hyperactivity
- ❖ Prevents destructive behaviour
- ❖ Builds strong relationships
- ❖ Geriatric dogs experience fewer or slower senile changes

GAMES

When we play games with our dogs, we give them the stimulation they need, make life more interesting and partake in a mutually enjoyable experience. We form a much better bond with them and they will be more attentive and focused on us. Playing games is a great way to phase out food rewards or as a reinforcer for training.

It is a good idea to have a few toys that are specifically for interactive games between you and your dog. Keep them for this purpose and only produce them when you want to play a game with your dog.

These interactive toys become really special, as they only have access to them when enjoying 'buddy' games. It will also allow you some control over when and where games take place and gives a clear signal to your dog that the game is on.

The level of control over games is important.

If we exert too much control, it may reduce enthusiasm and can put your dog off. She/he will lose interest quite quickly.

If we do not control the game enough, your dog may become over-stimulated and the situation can get out of hand.

Dogs have to be taught the rules of the game. Success breeds success. By making the goal achievable and giving the minimal amount of intervention, you can build confidence and

- -

enjoyment for your dog and increase his enthusiasm for the game.

Scenting and tracking games

The sense of smell is the most developed and important of the senses.

Dogs use their incredible olfactory abilities to interpret their environment; the sense of smell dominates their brain.

Channelling this ability into shared fun activities is highly stimulating and enjoyable for dogs, is a good bonding activity and one that dogs take to with great enthusiasm.

Indoors

Begin by putting your dog in a sit. Sit on the floor and let them watch as you drag a toy along the ground and tuck it out of sight behind you.

Try to direct him to the scent trail you laid. He should find it quite easily and be able to follow it to the target toy. Mark and reward when they achieve the goal.

Keep the finds relatively easy to begin with, then try going around the room and pretending to hide it in different locations, leaving it in one of them so that she/he has to search a bit harder to find the target.

Develop and expand as your dog gets the hang of the game.

Dogs are quite capable of distinguishing between different toys, so you can begin to teach the names of the toys.

Start by hiding two toys at the same time and ask him to find a specific toy, only mark and reward the right choice. Over time this can be built up to include several toys.

In this way the game evolves. The more challenging the game and the more your dog has to think, the more enjoyment and benefit your dog will get out of the game.

Outdoors –

The find the toy game can be expanded by putting your dog in a sit/stay (with assistance if necessary), move a short distance away, dragging your feet along the ground. Place the toy at the end of the trail and retrace your steps, being careful to backtrack along your original path. This will make it easier for your dog as he only has a single scent trail to follow.

Direct your dog to the scent trail you laid down and observe how well they are able to trace your path to the target.

Again this can be expanded, from short distances, to longer ones, then laying a path that curves etc. and after some practise it will no longer be necessary for you to drag your feet along the ground.

If at any stage your dog has difficulty making the finds, backtrack and decrease the difficulty, always try to give the least amount of assistance to enable them to achieve the finds on their own.

Hide and Seek

Hide and seek is an expansion on the 'find' games; play this in the house, garden and when out for walks.

The person that is hiding can lay a good scent trail down by dragging their feet to begin with, and make the finds fairly easy, until your dog is getting the hang of the game. The person that is hiding rewards the dog when they are found. Children really enjoy taking part in this fun activity.

Find Games with Food

Throw treats off the path for your dog to find while walking or out in the garden. This is a great game for improving focus.

Show your dog a treat, get them to sit. Wait until your dog is focused on the treat then throw it quite close to your dog to begin with to teach them the game. She/he should see it land and find it quite easily.

Repeat this a few times, always show the treat first and wait until your dog is focused before throwing. This is a fantastic distraction and focusing technique when you are out with your dog. You can build this up so that eventually you can throw a treat quite a distance into long grass and watch how much your dog enjoys tracking it down.

I play this often with my dogs when I am out. All I have to do is say 'pay attention' and my dogs instantly focus as they know that a find game is on!

Find the treat using 3 upturned yoghurt pots or plastic beakers and one treat. When your dog signals the right pot, she/he gets the prize!

You can also play hide the treat in the same way as the scent tracking games with toys, as outlined previously.

Catch, chase and retrieve

Most dogs enjoy one, or all of these games. These types of games channel your dogs natural chase instincts into something positive.

To keep it interesting, alternate between different types of toys; a Frisbee will act in a completely different way to a ball when thrown. Some toys, for instance the frame ball or Kong feeding toys, are designed to bounce at unpredictable angles on impact; which makes them more interesting and increases your dog's turn responses.

We can also stimulate them to think and make choices by throwing two toys at the same time, sometimes in the same direction, sometimes in opposite directions. As with all games you must retain a level of control.

Always ask for an action such as sit or down before throwing the toy. In this way game play helps to reinforce basic obedience and is used as a reward for good behaviour, while helping to reduce over-stimulation.

You should teach your dog to release a toy on command (see teaching 'drop'). Resist the temptation to chase your dog to retrieve the toy – this is a different game altogether and not one that should be encouraged!

For dogs that love water, floatation toys can be used when down at the beach, river or lake for water retrieval. There are several types on the market, or you can use just about anything of appropriate size that floats.

Tug of War

Many dogs enjoy a game of tug of war, it is a good activity for dogs that have a stronger kill instinct, so terriers and hunting dogs particularly enjoy this activity. This game is only suitable for fully mature dogs.

Many trainers still insist that you should never play tug games with your dog, because if you let him 'win' he thinks he is stronger than you and assumes the dominant position. As discussed earlier dogs do not think or behave in this way. In actual fact you are working with the dog, not against him in this game and letting him win occasionally increases enjoyment.

It is important to have a good grounding in 'take it' and 'drop' commands to give you some control of the game.

Alternating play between 'tug of war', chase and retrieve and mixing in some basic training along the way, helps you to keep control and will prevent your dog getting over excited.

If during a game of tug of war, your dog catches your hand with his teeth, end the game immediately. Your dog will soon learn that teeth on hands = end of game.

SELF REWARDING ACTIVITIES

Controlled self-rewarding activities are particularly good if you are leaving your dog unattended, or want them to amuse themselves in a constructive way.

Feeding Toys

Channel your dog's problem solving skills by getting them to work harder for their food.

Feeding toys are fantastic for engaging the brain. They come in all shapes and sizes; my particular preference is the Kong feeding toy. These good quality firm rubber toys have a larger hole in one end and a small hole in the other. When not in use as a feeding toy the shape of the Kong is designed to bounce at unpredictable angles, making them an interesting chase toy.

WARNING make sure that feeding toys have at least two holes. Feeding toys that only have one opening can cause the tongue to get trapped by suction and swell which is highly dangerous and can be fatal.

Stuffing – Drop something tasty in the bottom of the toy, such as a small amount of scraps, grated cheese or a few treats, then fill up with your dog's normal food. Your dog will smell the nice treats through the small hole, giving them an incentive to get the toy emptied.

If you pack it too tight your dog will not be able to gain success and will be put off the game, so when filling make sure it is quite loose; bits should start falling out as soon as you put it down. Once they have snuffled up the loose food, they will have to employ problem solving skills and different tactics to get the rest of the food out. You could give a stuffed feeding toy to many different dogs and they would each come up with their own unique system of getting it emptied.

In summer you can make an ice pop with a Kong. Plug the small hole with peanut butter and stand up in a freezer-proof cup. Fill with food, top it up with meat, chicken or fish stock and place in the freezer until frozen.

Balls

Balls can be self-rewarding because when dogs engage with them they have their own momentum, which stimulates further engagement.

For safety and to prevent a choke hazard, make sure you choose a size that is suitable for your dog. The variety is considerable between different sizes and textures, balls with bells inside that add audible stimulation. Footballs are great outdoor toys, but do puncture quite easily so a good alternative is a hard plastic boomer ball.

Squeaky Toys

Squeaky toys are 'kill' toys, the sound they produce imitates prey.

These are entertaining for dogs with a stronger predatory drive such as terriers and hunting breeds but any dog can enjoy them. There are many varieties of size, shape and texture, so a mixture will add interest.

My husky particularly likes soft cuddly squeaky toys; he will keep himself amused for a considerable time. The vinyl plastic toys however only last a few seconds before he dismantles them. So choose toys that are suitable and safe for your dog.

Rope Toys

Rope toys are a big favourite with my own dogs. They throw them up in the air and catch them, shake and worry them, shred them and play tug of war with each other.

They are also good for retrieval dogs who like to carry them around and greet you with them on your return.

Chewing

Chewing is not only important for teeth, gums and jaw muscles, but also the act of chewing produces Dopamine (the happy hormone) in the brain. Chewing is important for all dogs; it will calm highly strung dogs, relieve stress in anxious dogs and provide a pleasant and enjoyable activity to occupy them.

There are many different types of chew toys on the market, from really hard nylon bones to hard rubber toys of all shapes and sizes.

Hide chews (not suitable for young puppies) – These come in all shapes and sizes, and last a long time. If your dog doesn't eat it all in one session, remove it, and give it back to them the next time you want to occupy them. Make sure you pick a size that is suitable for your dog, if it is too big they might be put off; if it is too small it could be a choke hazard.

Pigs' Ears – Dogs love these, they are not very time consuming, particularly for bigger breeds, but they will enjoy them all the same.

If your dog has access to the same chew items all the time, they may get bored with them. It is better to put them away and choose the most beneficial times to give them, picking a different item each time.

To add interest, smear something tempting on them for example cream cheese or pate.

ENVIRONMENTAL INTEREST

Stimulate your dog's natural instincts by enriching the environment to supply some interesting activities.

Paddling Pools

Many breeds were developed to work in and around water and so are particularly partial to this activity; spaniels, retrievers, poodles and the Newfoundland to name a few.

However many dogs can enjoy water. If your dog is in to every puddle, river and stream, give them their own water source in the garden by adding a paddling pool.

You can purchase hard plastic pools for children that are ideal for your dog. Add floatation toys for extra interest.

Sand Pits

For dogs who love to dig, give them their own place to enjoy their hobby. (Problem digging is covered in Section 6)

You can build a raised pit using shuttered wood or use a hard plastic paddling pool for children and fill with sand.

Bury some toys or treats for extra interest.

Foraging

There is nothing stimulating about getting free food in a dish every day.

Make food more interesting by scattering and hiding it so your dog has to not only forage but also engage their problem solving skills to gain it. You could put some under an overturned plant pot, place some in a sealed envelope under the mat, or hide a stuffed feeding toy in their bed. If you have time and don't mind clearing up you can put food into small cereal boxes and tape them up, then hide the parcel. They will have to find it and problem solve to retrieve the food; the more inventive you are the more your dog will enjoy the activity.

Always make it reasonably easy to start with so they can gain success and build enjoyment and confidence in the game.

STIMULATING WALKS

Obviously walking our dogs regularly is essential, but it is not just about physical exercise, it is also an important source of mental stimulation.

As human beings we tend to rely mainly on sight to interpret a new environment, for dogs it is their sense of smell.

Dogs gather a vast array of information through their olfactory abilities and often you will see your dog following a scent trail with great enthusiasm.

Other dogs leave traces of pheromones through scent glands in their feet, urine and faeces. Dogs can gather detailed information, whether the animal is male or female, neutered or entire, socially dominant or submissive and even the state of their health.

It is comparable to you finding and browsing through a strangers CV and learning something about that individual. Not only is it their most important sense but as mentioned earlier it also dominates their brain.

As stated previously there is a vast difference between the scent receptors in humans and dogs:-

- ❖ Humans - 5 million
- ❖ Terriers -147 million
- ❖ German shepherd -225 million
- ❖ Bloodhounds - 300 million

A dog's scenting ability is incredible and difficult for us to imagine. Compared to dogs, our sense of smell is virtually non existent.

Exiting your gate and walking your dog around the block every evening; while good physical exercise, has minimal stimulation. It is comparable to enjoying a TV show, but only watching repeats of the same episode over and over again.

Therefore, varying the types of locations where we exercise our dogs creates more interest and increases mental stimulation. Town parks, beach, woodlands, lakes, hill walking, country and town walks, variety is the spice of life!

Long lead and off lead walks are particularly beneficial, as they allow dogs to really explore their environment. These types of walks are suitable for areas where it is permitted and safe. Obviously you must have a good level of training and control before you allow your dog off the lead.

While under training, or in public areas where dogs have to be kept on the lead, extendable leads are ideal, as you can give your dog freedom, while still retaining control.

The standard length of extendable lead is usually 16 feet, but there are extra long leads on the market which extend out to 26 feet which are even better. (Please refer to safety warnings on Page 111).

TRAINING – EXPAND ON THE BASICS

Training should be an ongoing experience and can provide fun and stimulation.

Using positive reinforcement, daily sessions of basic obedience and teaching new and interesting things through play/training, is a good way of spending quality time, improving obedience and building a strong relationship between you and your dog.

Make training fun and interesting by varying the activities and encouraging your dog to explore their natural instincts.

Dogs are unique individuals and different dogs will enjoy different activities. It is best to concentrate on the areas where your dog excels, thus encouraging his natural talents and increasing enjoyment. The more varied the training the more stimulating and rewarding for your dog.

Dogs are capable of learning many commands, so expand on the basics. Once you have mastered the principal of positive reinforcement training and have practised teaching your dog some basic commands, try using the same methods to teach new skills and tricks; this is only limited by your imagination.

JUMP THROUGH A HOOP

If your dog is under 18 months, keep the jumps low (only a few inches) as you can cause damage to developing joints.

To teach your dog to jump through a hula hoop using lure and reward methods is simple and fun. Hold the hoop upright with the base on the floor to begin with. Utilise an established 'touch' or offer a treat or a toy to lure your dog through - Mark and reward if successful.

Practise getting your dog to go through in both directions. When you have a few successful repeats, introduce a command as your dog goes through the hoop still using your lure. Then try using your hand without the lure using your command. When your dog is getting the hang of it you can raise it up an inch or two so they begin to jump through, it can then gradually be raised to an appropriate height for the age and breed of your dog.

This activity is a good precursor for the tyre jump in agility training.

SHUT THE DOOR

Teach your dog to shut the door using target training.

Choose a tub lid (from a gravy granule tub for instance) place it on the floor and let your dog watch as you place a treat underneath. Pin the target to the floor with your fingers.

- -

Your dog will offer different behaviour to get the treat, be patient, wait until your dog taps the target with a paw – mark the behaviour and remove the lid so they are rewarded with the treat.

Practise getting your dog to hit the target with their paw – always mark and reward when successful. You can then begin to work without the treat under the target, reinforcing the behaviour with your mark and reward with a treat from your hand.

When your dog is hitting the target with their paw reliably, move the target into your hand, keeping it parallel and close to the floor to begin with.

You can then gradually increase the height and adjust the angle so eventually your dog is tapping the target, no matter what height or angle it is offered. This should be done over several training sessions.

Once your dog is reliably tapping the target at different heights and positions, attach the target to a door with a piece of Blue-tack, making sure it is at the right height for your dog to reach. When you have had a few successful repeats of your dog tapping the target and pushing the door, you can introduce a 'door' command as he does it.

Once your dog is associating 'door' with the action of hitting the target with his foot and pushing the door, you can try removing the target. If you are not getting the desired results go back a stage.

This type of target training can, with a little imagination, be used to teach your dog many other types of tricks and activities.

TOYS IN THE BOX

Teach your dog to tidy up after himself by putting his toys away in a toy box.

As this is quite complicated, break the training down into sections. For example concentrate and practise teaching your dog to pick up a toy first - mark and reward the behaviour.

The next step - drop it in the box – hopefully your dog has already learnt the 'drop' command. Place the box under his chin and ask for the action. After a few successful repeats of the toy landing in the box, introduce an appropriate command as the action occurs.

The next stage is to put the box on the floor a few inches away and gradually increase the distance the dog has to travel to the box to drop the toy inside.

This type of training should be done in small stages over several training sessions.

SPORTS AND ACTIVITIES

For high energy owners, why not consider one of the dog sports that will not only keep you fit, but will allow your dog to get the exercise they need and participate in their favourite activities, while strengthening the bond between you.

This section outlines in brief some of the activities to consider. If you find a sport that you are interested in pursuing, it is worthwhile going to local events to talk to people who are involved in the sport and get a feel for what is involved.

InnerWolf in the UK and The Dog Outdoors in the USA both have a fantastic range of equipment for all dog sports activities and their staff are on hand to give expert advice should you need it.

Make sure that your dog has a reasonable level of training before participating in dog sports and activities.

No dog under a year should be pulling weight or partaking in agility as this can damage developing bones and joints, so these activities are only suitable for fully grown, healthy dogs.

Cold muscles are more prone to injury so it is important that both you and your dog warm up before participating in any of the following sports and allow a cool down period after the activities.

When starting out, keep sessions short to begin with, building up gradually as fitness and stamina increases.

Avoid running in hot weather, even in temperate climates, dogs can become dehydrated quite quickly, so always have water to hand and offer regularly.

Check the paws and pads of your dog both before and after activities to make sure there are no cuts or abrasions.

Warming up

At least ten minutes walking, during which time change direction regularly, you can utilise your 'touch' command to get your dog to turn half circles and full circles around you at walking pace.

After the walking warm up spend a few minutes massaging your dog's muscles, this increases the supply of oxygen rich blood to the muscles. Particular attention should be focused on the shoulders, triceps, neck, back and all the muscle groups in the back legs. While doing this, you will be stretching and warming up your own muscles!

Encouraging your dog to stretch can help to warm up tendons and ligaments. This should not be forced stretching, whereby you are physically manipulating the limbs as this can cause injury. Rather it should be voluntary stretching; dogs will only stretch as far as they feel comfortable. (This can be achieved by reinforcing the behaviour every time you see your dog stretching and associating a command to the action)

This can be followed by another 5 minutes of alternating between fast walking and trotting, with circling and direction changes at a faster pace.

Cooling Down

After activity, gradually slow to a walk for at least 5 minutes after running or until such time as your dog's breathing returns to normal and is no longer panting. Spend a few minutes massaging the muscles as before in the warm up and encourage your dog to do some gentle stretches. This cooling down period allows your dog's heart rate and respiration to return to normal.

Canicross

With the minimum of equipment, you and your dog can be up and running with Canicross, keep fit and give your dog the exercise they need!

Canicross is the sport of cross country running with your dog and is suitable for all breeds, both large and small that have reached maturity.

It can be a solitary sport or a social one, there are many groups that meet regularly for canicross fun and competition, so check your local area for details and spend some time with like minded people, while giving your dog an activity that they will love.

Equipment needed:

Waist belt with a 2 metre bungie line, this helps protect both you and your dog from sudden jarring, while the waist belt leaves your hands free.

Padded dog harness that spreads the load of the pull, without restricting movement.

Portable dish and water supply.

When starting out, it is best to choose a familiar environment, preferably with well defined paths. Avoid wide open spaces like beaches and open fields.

Build up gradually as fitness improves.

Bikejoring, Scootering, Skijoring and Rollerjoring

Not keen on running? There are other ways to share fun activities with your dog. Dog powered bikes, scooters, rollerskates and skis.

This is best suited to medium/larger breeds.

Before partaking in these activities it is advisable to have a good level of mushing/directional commands in place.

Before investing in equipment go to some local events, talk to people involved with the sport and get advice. If using more than one dog, spend time training each dog individually before putting them together as a team.

Always plan your route and know your environment, particularly when skijoring and rollerjoring, steep slopes and no brakes is not a good combination!

I would also strongly advise protective clothing, head protection, goggles (dogs can throw up debris that can cause eye injury) and gloves at the very least.

Dog Agility

Most dogs, both large and small can enjoy dog agility.

While agility equipment training is only suitable for fully mature dogs, some pre-agility training in directional control can begin earlier in preparation. The only equipement that is safe for younger dogs is the tunnel.

Agility equipment consists of:

- ❖ High Jumps
- ❖ Long Jump
- ❖ A Frame
- ❖ Dog Walk
- ❖ Weave Poles
- ❖ Tunnel
- ❖ See Saw
- ❖ Tyre Jump

Check out your local area for agility classes or alternatively, why not set up your own agility course in the garden.

Remember, training your dog on agility equipment (with the exception of the tunnel) should only be encouraged when your dog is physically mature.

BENEFITS IN THE TWILIGHT YEARS

There are many changes that affect dogs in later life. Apart from the physical changes to the major organs; sensory decline and stiffness, all of which can influence behaviour, dogs undergo changes in the brain that affect thought processes.

This occurs when the brain cells begin to break down; the filaments that transmit and receive information begin to shrink and lose contact with neighbouring cells.

The brain cells that are responsible for amplifying and refining signals remain stimulated for longer, which causes a jamming of information. This affects short-term memory as they are unable to process any further information while this is happening. Long-term memory is also affected due to a reduction of oxygen to the brain as the lungs become less efficient and blood vessels in the brain lose their elasticity. Other major changes in the brain include the thickening of the meninges and changes in the hypothalamus, which controls the hormonal system.

These changes influence behaviour, sleep patterns, learning ability and reaction times. We are unable to stop this process, but we are able to slow it down by ensuring our dogs have the physical and mental stimulation they need. Environment can affect the degeneration of the brain.

In an experiment at the University of Illinois, it was proved that it was possible to achieve a re-growth of the filaments that transmit and receive information in old animals. Old rats that had lived their lives in a dull and uninteresting environment were placed into cages with slides, wheels, ramps and other rats. They became more active, more sociable and seemed to enjoy life more. When the brains of these rats were compared to the rats left in the dull environment, it showed that on average the stimulated rats had 2000 more synapses in the cerebellum and a re-growth had occurred.

The brain is modified throughout life by environmental influences. By increasing stimulation we can influence the brain.

There is no doubt that a dog's environment can have a dramatic influence on the mind and by exercising and stimulating the senses and keeping the brain active, we can slow down natural deterioration and increase the oxygen supply to the brain, improving long-term memory.

By giving our dogs an active and mentally stimulating life, we can effectively slow down the ageing process and possibly even increase their lifespan. They would experience fewer or slower senile changes.

As the experiment showed it is never too late to increase stimulation, even in old dogs. It is possible to improve brain function even at this stage by giving our dogs a more interesting and active life.

Summary

Allowing dogs to partake and enjoy their natural behaviour and engage their brains in positive ways, can prevent and resolve many behaviour problems.

Playing games with dogs is a mutually enjoyable experience, builds strong and lasting bonds and provides essential mental stimulation.

Providing self- rewarding constructive activities curbs boredom – especially during home alone times.

Giving dogs a stimulating and active lifestyle can slow down the ageing process and the onset of brain degeneration in elderly dogs.

SECTION 6

DEALING WITH PROBLEM
BEHAVIOUR

Contributing Factors

Checklist for Solving Problems

Common Behavioural Problems in detail

Excessive Barking

Jumping up

Digging

Begging

Aggression

PROBLEM SOLVING

There are different reasons why people experience problems with their dog. It is not that dogs are acting abnormally; it is rather that the behaviour presented is inappropriate to a particular situation, is excessive or socially unacceptable.

In order to begin to resolve behavioural issues you must attempt to establish what is driving the behaviour; often the problem presented can be a symptom of something deeper. As well as tackling the symptom, changes may be needed to address the root cause to achieve long term success.

This section offers information to help diagnose possible causes of problem behaviour and encourages you to consider what action may be needed in order to resolve them.

The most common contributing factors:-

❖ Inadequate or inconsistent training
❖ The dog has learned that the behaviour is rewarding
❖ The behaviour is self-rewarding
❖ Lack of exercise and/or mental stimulation.
❖ The choice of breed may not be appropriate for the owner's lifestyle, circumstances or expectations.

Behaviour problems can also be caused by:-

- ❖ Stress and anxiety
- ❖ An underlying medical condition
- ❖ Nutritional affects

- -

CHECK LIST FOR PROBLEM SOLVING

If you are experiencing problems with your dog's behaviour, you should ask yourself the following questions:-

Has there been a change in normal behaviour patterns that may indicate an underlying medication condition?

For example: -

Dogs that were housetrained begin to have accidents in the house. This may be a urinary tract, bladder or kidney infection.

Not enjoying, slowing down or refusing to go out for walks - There may be pain in the joints, muscles or ligaments.

Sudden onset of aggression - this may include growling, snarling, lunging or biting. This may be due to illness, pain or sensory decline.

If you notice any sudden changes in your dog's *normal* behaviour, get them checked out thoroughly by your vet.

Is your dog showing signs of stress or anxiety?

There maybe one or more of the following signs that could indicate your dog may be suffering from stress: -

- ❖ salivating
- ❖ pacing
- ❖ panting (when not exercising or hot)
- ❖ yawning
- ❖ licking the lips
- ❖ hyperactivity
- ❖ excessive barking
- ❖ obsessive digging
- ❖ escape behaviour
- ❖ destructive behaviour

If you suspect that your dog is displaying stress related behaviour, it is advisable to consult a professional to help you. This is a specialist area and a behaviourist will be able to assess areas that may be contributing to stress/anxiety, and be able to recommend a course of appropriate action.

Am I responding to the behaviour in a way that is rewarding the dog?

Remember that trying to actively teach your dog that a particular behaviour is wrong, may be reinforcing the behaviour.

If the problem is getting progressively worse, it is probably because the dog finds the behaviour rewarding in some way.

Examine how you are reacting to the problem and try adjusting your approach. Consider what other positive counter productive actions can be encouraged.

Is there an alternative behaviour that I could encourage that is counterproductive to the problem?

For example if your dog is sitting, this is counterproductive to jumping up.

If your dog is prone to 'mouthing' (grabbing your hand with their mouth) encourage them to hold a toy in their mouth, or teach the 'touch' command as a positive alternative.

Is there an alternative environment or situation in which the behaviour can be encouraged, that is acceptable?

If your dog enjoys digging up your garden plants, can you supply a sand pit for digging as an acceptable alternative?

If your dog chases everything that moves, birds, bikes, people – channel their chase instincts into something positive like toy retrieval.

Can I control the environment to prevent the behaviour occurring?

For instance, if your dog regularly destroys your mail - restrict access to the hallway or fit a basket on the letter box to catch the mail.

If your dog is raiding the bin, replace with a more tamper proof bin or place the bin in an inaccessible place such as a closed room or inside a cupboard to prevent access.

Is your dog getting enough exercise and mental stimulation?

Many problem behaviours are caused by boredom, lack of exercise or mental stimulation. Dogs are intelligent, if we do not stimulate them enough they will invent their own entertainment. This may include barking, digging, escape behaviour, pulling washing off the line and general destruction to name but a few. (These can also be signs of stress if excessive)

Give your dog more frequent and stimulating walks and increase environmental interest and mental stimulation.

Is your dog on a good quality and appropriate diet?

Many dogs can have an adverse reaction to food containing colours, poor quality food, food allergies or intolerances which can cause hyperactivity, pica (eating faeces and other non food items) scratching and skin problems and other behavioural problems. If you suspect that the diet is affecting your dog, seek advice from your veterinary surgeon or qualified behaviourist for advice on trying an elimination diet to establish if the diet is contributing to the behaviour.

Am I equipped to deal with the problem?

Never be afraid to ask for professional help.

- -

For serious problems such as aggression, do not delay; contact a qualified behaviourist to help you immediately. The sooner it can be diagnosed and treated – the better.

If you have tried and failed to rectify less serious behaviour problems, seek help from a professional dog trainer or behaviourist. Seek recommendations from other dog owners or your veterinary surgeon and don't be afraid to ask questions regarding their qualifications, experience and training methods before engaging someone to help you.

Reliable professionals will be quite happy to answer any questions you have. Only engage professional help from individuals who use positive reinforcement methods and avoid trainers that suggest your dog's training or behaviour issue are due to dominance issues.

Summary

Has there been a change in normal behaviour patterns that may have an underlying medical condition?

Is your dog showing signs of stress and anxiety?

Am I responding in a way that is rewarding the behaviour?

Is there an alternative behaviour that I could encourage that is counterproductive to the problem?

Is there a situation that the behaviour can be encouraged that is acceptable?

Can the environment be controlled to prevent the behaviour occurring?

Is your dog getting enough exercise and mental stimulation?

Is your dog on an appropriate diet?

Am I equipped to deal with the problem?

- -

COMMON BEHAVIOURAL PROBLEMS

In this section we will look at some common behavioural problems, possible causes and solutions.

EXCESSIVE BARKING

Barking is normal dog behaviour and in some situations we want our dogs to alert us, protect us or to let us know that they may need to be let out for a toilet break.

Excessive or persistent vocalisation however is not only annoying for your own household, but can lead to conflict with neighbours.

Physical punishment or aversive training techniques that utilise pain, shock or fear should not be used. You should never punish your dog for expressing natural behaviour.

There are devices on the market- Anti-Bark collars that punish dogs by delivering an electric shock or a squirt of foul smelling spray whenever they bark. You should never use these types of aversive training devices; you are indiscriminately punishing your dog for exhibiting natural behaviour which can lead to psychological damage.

Imagine how you would feel if you received the same treatment every time you tried to talk. These methods will cause pain, anxiety or fear and lead to other more serious problems.

Consider your choice of breed. If you are leaving your dog unattended while at work, it is best to avoid breeds that have a predisposition to bark. Terriers and toy breeds can be persistent barkers, hunting hounds and beagles have a high volume bay, and husky breeds can be vocal, particularly when left alone. Excessive barking is not always genetically inherent; any dog can present this problem.

Outside of a genetic predisposition, the most common causes for persistent barking could include:-

Boredom, lack of exercise and mental stimulation, social isolation

If this is the route of the problem, the solution is to give your dog a more active and stimulating life. If you are not in a position to exercise your dog enough, think about engaging a professional dog walker or a family member to help you.

If your dog is being left for long periods of time, try and walk them before leaving, and/or arrange for someone to break their day up with a walk or a play session.

Make the environment more stimulating and interesting to give them positive things to occupy them when left alone as outlined previously.

Visual and Audible Stimulation

Some dogs will bark when they see and hear things that stimulate them.

If you are living in a busy area, this can be problematic. Often I have seen dogs perched on top of the couch or window sill, watching the world go by and barking constantly.

In this case environmental changes are needed.

For indoor dogs: Try and prevent access to areas where the dog is able to see out of a window. Move furniture that the dog is using to gain a high vantage point, or draw the blinds or curtains to prevent the dog seeing out.

Leave a radio on for background noise to help mask noises from outside.

Make the environment more interesting, and give them something more stimulating and rewarding to focus on.

For outdoor dogs: If the dog is allowed access to the front of the house where all the action is, try and move them around the back where it is a bit quieter. Make the environment more interesting, and give them something else more stimulating and rewarding to do.

Attention Seeking or Learned Behaviour

Dogs have different types and tones of bark.

The sharp bark that they give when they want to alert us, is quite different from the bark they use when playing or attention seeking. Obviously sometimes we want to pay attention if they are trying to alert us.

Take note of the different sounds your dog makes in different situations. If, every time your dog barks, no matter what the type of sound they are using you give them your full attention, you may be rewarding the behaviour. This could include shouting at them, getting up to see what they want, throwing a toy or giving them treats to occupy them so you can get some peace. The dog learns that to get attention or a reward on demand, they only have to bark. The behaviour will become more frequent and more persistent.

Remember if you reward behaviour, it becomes stronger and more frequent. The best course of action is a combination of the following:-

Ignoring the behaviour when appropriate i.e. attention seeking bark - do not look at, speak to or otherwise engage. If the problem has built up over a period of time, you could use a 'time out'. As soon as the dog begins the behaviour, say nothing, either remove him from room or remove yourself from the dog.

Teach your dog to stop barking on command

Spend some time actively teaching your dog to stop barking on command.

Using the same mark and reward techniques as previously explained, wait until your dog stops barking – mark and reward. Each time they bark, wait until they stop – mark and reward. After a few repetitions, begin to introduce a verbal command, you could use 'quiet' or 'sshhhh'. Once your dog is associating the command with the action, try giving your command while they are barking and then wait until they stop – mark and reward.

Even when your dog has alerted you to an impending visitor, once you are aware of the situation you want them to stop when told.

Stress or Anxiety

When dogs are stressed or anxious they can engage in displacement activities. This is where they exhibit normal dog behaviour in excess.

Constant or excessive barking can be one symptom of stress. If you think your dog maybe barking because of stress, you do not need to address the symptom (barking), you need to work with your dog to reduce stress. By reducing stress the problem barking will improve.

Seek help from a professional if you think that this may be the case.

JUMPING UP

When we bring home our lovely bundle of fluff, they are so adorable, cute and small. They jump up on us and we cannot help but OOhh and AAhh, pick them up and cuddle them.

Puppy is exhibiting normal behaviour, but is learning every time she/he gets this lovely response that it is also a rewarding behaviour, they will respond by jumping up more and more often.

Encouraging your dog to jump up can result in damage to hips, joints and ligaments in the developing dog which can have long-term health implications.

Puppy is going to grow quite rapidly, the cute jumping up behaviour is quickly going to become at best antisocial, inconvenient and embarrassing (especially when visitors call) and at worst potentially dangerous and frightening, particularly for children, people who are nervous of dogs and the older generation.

What usually happens at this juncture – owners now decide to teach their dog that this is wrong.

The most common mistakes when trying to teach dogs not to jump up:

Shouting – I have often seen owners shouting in sentences as if to explain that this is not acceptable behaviour and it is expected that the dog should understand. This response is rewarding and can cause dogs to become even more excited and out of control. She/he is still getting a huge response for the

- -

behaviour; it is a different response to the pick me up and cuddle me, but rewarding none the less.

Pushing them off – This turns the whole thing into a game that increases excitement. Dogs will match their response with equal force to their opponent in play, so you will find that the harder you push a dog away, the harder it will return. As we know, games are rewarding for dogs and a good reinforcer for behaviour. This response is exciting and stimulating and will make the behaviour even worse.

Obviously if we treat the behaviour correctly from the beginning, jumping up will stop quickly and easily. The longer the behaviour has been encouraged the more effort it takes to extinguish.

This is achieved by:-

❖ Ignoring the behaviour
❖ Teaching an alternative behaviour that is counterproductive and more rewarding
❖ Controlling the behaviour
❖ 100% consistency

Let's look at each stage in more detail:

Ignore the behaviour

I often say to owners, if your dog only has two feet on the ground, it turns into an invisible dog.

If your dog jumps up at you, avoid eye contact, make sure you also turn your face away and use your body language to your advantage, cross your arms and turn away.

From the dog's perspective if jumping up results in no response there is little point in doing it so the behaviour will gradually extinguish.

Try and make a point of giving your dog lots of attention if they come up to you without jumping up. Reward the behaviour you want to encourage.

Teach a more rewarding alternative

You will not be successful by just ignoring the behaviour; we must also reward the dog when they are behaving in a more acceptable way. To begin with, as soon as your dog returns to all four feet, mark and reward.

As discussed previously for retraining and reshaping behaviour, clicker training works well and is particularly effective for this problem as it is a calm marker.

If you go to reward your dog and she/he immediately returns to jumping, you must withdraw the reward and turn away immediately.

One of the best counterproductive behaviours to encourage as a positive alternative; is the sit. (See Teaching the Basics.) If your dog is sitting it is not jumping up, so really concentrate on teaching and rewarding this behaviour. The more you reward it, the stronger it will become.

Control the behaviour

If there is an existing problem with jumping up, you will need to take this extra measure.

When receiving visitors do not allow your dog to greet them at the door; secure him/her in another room.

Let your visitors come in and sit down. Instruct them to ignore your dog until she/he is calm.

Put your dog on the lead and spend a minute practising sit and some focusing exercises such as hand touches. This will help to focus and calm your dog before you give them access to your visitors. Bring them into the room and wait until your dog has got over their initial excitement. Mark and reward calm behaviour.

If your dog comes into the room and is hyperactive and doesn't begin to settle in a reasonable amount of time, say nothing, turn them around and take them out again. Begin the process again.

Once you can bring them in and get them focused and calm, gradually work them closer to the visitors until you are able to control their behaviour up close. You can then mark calm behaviour and the visitors can give the reward. Once you are happy that your dog is calm you can drop the lead, but if she/he jumps up, say nothing, pick up the lead and remove from the room immediately.

If your dog remains calm for a few minutes, you can take the lead off. Once you have mastered this, you can, if you wish, bring your dog to the door on the lead to greet visitors, using exactly the same approach.

100% Consistency

This is absolutely crucial!

Once you begin to deal with this problem, you must be vigilant. If you have been ignoring the behaviour and then you forget yourself and respond to it, this is an intermittent reward and as discussed previously, intermittent rewards strengthen behaviour making dogs work harder to gain the reward.

The other problem can be lack of support by other family members. If you are being consistent, but someone else in the household is not, your dog will learn not to jump up on you but will still jump up on other people (including visitors and strangers) to test if that person will reward them. You will never stop your dog jumping up on people.

WARNING - For dogs that have previously been encouraged to jump up and are under retraining, there is a possibility that the problem may initially get worse before it gets better. If dogs are used to being rewarded for behaviour and they suddenly get no reward, they may try a new and even worse behaviour. For instance they may try jumping up and barking, or jumping up and scraping with their paw.

It is essential that you do not inadvertently reinforce this new behaviour by responding.

DIGGING

If you are reading this section it probably means that your garden, a once lovingly tended landscape, now looks as if it has been attacked by giant moles! While we might love our dogs, we do not always appreciate their idea of landscape gardening.

Not only can this be a behaviour issue, it can also cause arguments and conflict between family members. "Have your seen what *your* dog has done to *my* garden!"

Before you get to the stage of needing a marriage guidance counsellor, let us look at some possible causes and solutions.

Why do dogs dig?

Hobby diggers and genetic predisposition

This instinct is hard wired into certain breeds, short legged Terriers and Dachshunds were bred to dig out small prey, so have a genetic predisposition for this behaviour. Hunting hounds can also have a strong tendency to dig as do husky type dogs. It is not just these breeds however, mixed breed dogs and any other breed of dog can enjoy digging.

You cannot prevent digging behaviour in some dogs, but don't despair there are measures you can take to preserve your garden. The way to achieve this is to allocate an area of the garden where they have permission to dig, allowing them to enjoy their hobby while saving the rest of your garden from destruction.

Choose a spot, preferably with some shade, allow as big an area as you can afford to give. Build a raised box using wood shuttering, or buy a child's plastic paddling pool and fill it with sand. Sand is preferable to mud, as it is cleaner, will dry quicker after rain and is easier for the dog to shake off.

Collect some of their favourite toys and some tasty treats. Take your dog to the area, and let him watch you bury the goodies; chances are he'll be digging them up quicker than you can bury them.

As soon as he begins to dig in the sand, mark and reward.

To begin with you will need to supervise time in the garden, if she/he starts to dig in the sandbox mark and reward. If she/he digs anywhere else, put them on the lead, and bring them in. Leave it for a few minutes, take them back out to the sand box and encourage them to dig there instead.

Always praise when you see him digging in his area and bury something tasty or of interest in his sand box every day for the first week and regularly thereafter.

Your dog will learn that digging in his special area is more rewarding than digging elsewhere as you have positively reinforced the behaviour and they have discovered something tasty or interesting buried in that area, which is also self-rewarding.

Rewarding digging behaviour in that one spot strengthens the behaviour; removing him from the garden for inappropriate digging, weakens the behaviour.

Temperature control

Heavy coated dogs that originated in colder climates (Samoyed, huskies, Pyrenees, Newfoundland and dogs in the Spitz group for example), tend to have dense double coats which consist of an inner downy coat, and an outer coat of guard hairs that act as weather protection.

These breeds can suffer in the heat. If you notice your dog is only digging in warmer weather and lying in the excavated hole, it is probably to create a cool place to lie in.

In this case digging is not for pleasure but for comfort.

You can prevent this type of digging by making sure there are plenty of shady areas in the garden using large shrubs, trees or fencing, and by adding a paddling pool. You can purchase hard plastic children's paddling pools (obviously inflatable pools are not suitable!) fill with water and place in a shady area of the garden. Always make sure there is a fresh bowl of drinking water available.

Never leave dogs outside in hot weather with no shade or water, as there is a danger of heat stroke.

Boredom and lack of Mental Stimulation

Digging is an option if there is nothing better on offer to do. If you think your dog is digging out of boredom, make the environment more interesting and increase mental stimulation with activities previously described.

Lack of exercise/high energy.

Digging is an effective way of expending excess energy and is one way dogs can exercise themselves if they lack other physical activity.

If this is the case either increase the amount of walks, or change the type of walks to either off lead (if suitably trained) or extendable lead walks, which allows dogs more freedom to exercise and explore than short lead walks.

Another way of expending some of your dog's physical energy is through game play. Fetch, chase, retrieve games are ideal.

Check your dog's diet to make sure that they are on an appropriate level of protein. High protein diets can cause excessive energy levels, so this may also be a contributing factor.

Displacement Activity/Escape behaviour

If digging is obsessive, it may be a symptom of stress, particularly if they are showing other symptoms.

If this is the case you need to treat the cause, not the symptom. If you think that stress may be a factor, seek professional help.

BEGGING

Begging is a learned behaviour.

Prevention is better than cure, it is better not to teach your dog to beg by never feeding from your plate or the table.

Once learnt this can become a nuisance and a source of embarrassment, especially when you have visitors. It can range from mild behaviour, staring, pacing from one person to another or drooling (sometimes with head on laps under the table) to more proactive behaviour such as persistent whining, barking, pawing and climbing up on people or jumping up at the table.

However the behaviour presents itself is testimony to what has worked in the past. More extreme behaviour usually results when people have attempted to rectify mild begging behaviour by stopping feeding from the table, but have not been consistent. When dogs are used to getting a reward and it suddenly stops, they will try increasingly demanding behaviour until they find a behaviour that works.

Possible solutions could include:

Implement a strict family rule

No feeding from the table or plate and ignoring begging behaviour: In order for this to work it must be a 100% commitment with no exceptions.

With some family situations this may be difficult to implement as one or more members may be unable to resist, especially if the behaviour escalates as the dog tries new tactics.

At this point someone may give in; either because they feel sorry for the dog or they find the new behaviour intolerable and find it easier to give in to stop the behaviour. This reinforces the behaviour and makes the problem worse.

If you can't get the whole family on board you will have to restrict your dog's access at meal times.

Prevent Access

Put your dog into a separate room with their own dinner while the family eats theirs, or if you use a crate for your dog, put them in the crate with something positive to do before sitting down to dinner.

Teach a more rewarding alternative

Encourage a more rewarding behaviour that is counterproductive.

Teach your dog to perform a behaviour that can be positively reinforced and is incompatible with begging, for example going to his bed or mat.

AGGRESSION

Aggression in dogs is defined as a threatening or harmful behaviour directed toward another living creature.

This includes snarling, growling, snapping, lunging and biting. Dogs that show such behaviour are not abnormal; they are merely exhibiting normal dog behaviour.

As discussed previously, growling and/or showing teeth is a way for dogs to let us know that they are not coping with a situation. By this time, many other body language cues have been missed, and they have had to resort to stronger indications.

Dogs should never be punished for growling. This is a normal part of canine communication and a clear warning that if pressed, a bite may follow.

If dogs become afraid to growl because they have been punished for it in the past, we end up with a potentially dangerous situation. A dog will bypass these strong warning signals and go straight for the bite.

There are different types of aggression: fear, predatory, inter-dog, territorial, resource guarding, maternal, pain related or redirected aggression.

The lines are sometimes not definable to one particular type of aggression. For instance dogs can be territorially aggressive with elements of fear; redirected aggression can occur if a dog is interrupted

- -

when it is in a heightened state due to other types of aggression, such as inter-dog or territorial aggression.

What ever the cause, aggression is a serious matter and mismanagement can cause an escalation or result in injury.

Always seek help from a qualified behaviourist.

SECTION 7

IF AND WHEN TO NEUTER

Neutering and Weight Gain

Neutering Males

Optimal time to Neuter

Implications of Neutering too Early

Neutering older Dogs

Spaying Females

Implications of Spaying too Early

NEUTERING INFORMATION

There are different schools of thought regarding neutering. It can be confusing for owners to make an informed decision as to the right age to get their dog neutered, or indeed whether they should get them neutered at all.

Neutering has many health and behavioural benefits, as well as helping to reduce the number of unwanted dogs destroyed each year.

However, it is important to consider the timing of such procedures in order to reap the maximum benefit and reduce the risk of detrimental health problems if neutering is carried out too early.

Neutering and Weight Gain

This is one concern that many people have in connection to neutering their dogs.

It is true to say that some dogs may experience changes in their metabolism after neutering. This is not a problem in itself. Weight gain may occur however if the feeding levels remain the same. Therefore, it is important to monitor dogs post neutering as it may be necessary to adjust food intake to balance out metabolic changes.

Often it is just a case of a slight reduction of the amount of daily food given to prevent weight gain.

NEUTERING MALES

Castrated males are less likely to be aggressive or be aggressed upon by other male dogs and will be less likely to roam. It also removes the risk of testicular cancer.

Unneutered mature male dogs will scent mark which can contribute to house training problems. This behaviour is not connected to the need to empty their bladder; rather they will leave small splashes of urine in strategic areas to mark territory.

This is why male dogs 'cock' their leg, so that urine traces are left at nose level for other dogs and will not be missed. This behaviour begins when testosterone levels begin to rise and they reach sexual maturity. The age that this occurs varies from dog to dog.

Puppies and juvenile males squat until such time as their testosterone levels begin to rise.

Optimal Time to Neuter Male Dogs

Development times will vary between individuals. For this reason, it is inadvisable to specify that males should be neutered at a specific age.

The optimum time for the neutering of males is when they first begin to tentatively lift their leg when urinating. This shows that the testosterone levels of the particular dog are rising and he is becoming sexually mature.

If neutering occurs at this time it will reap the maximum benefits, prevent the development of scent marking behaviour and other testosterone related issues such as inter dog aggression and roaming.

Implications of Neutering Too Early

Physical – Males that are castrated before reaching maturity, often grow taller than they should, as the lack of dihydrotestosterone fails to signal the cessation of bone growth at the normal time.

This can result in dogs that are too long in the leg and can cause disproportionate growth between the fore and hind legs, putting pressure on the skeletal structure, in particular the hips and spine.

There also seems to be some evidence of a link between osteosarcoma (bone cancer) and prepubescent castration in male dogs.

Behavioural – From a behavioural perspective, my own observations over the course of many years suggest that neutering males before they mature has the effect of 'locking' dogs into a juvenile psychological state. This can result in dogs that do not develop emotional maturity, remain 'giddy' and retain a shorter attention span.

Neutering Older Dogs

Behavioural benefits of castration reduce if surgery is carried out when dogs are well in to maturity.

In the case of scent marking for example, although testosterone was the driving force behind the original behaviour, it soon becomes normal behaviour for the dog.

Consequently if the behaviour has become well established, reduction of testosterone due to castration may have little or no effect.

Although there may be other benefits of later neutering, behaviour problems associated with high testosterone may not improve following the procedure.

SPAYING FEMALES

Spaying female dogs involves the surgical removal of the uterus and ovaries.

In bitches neutering can dramatically reduce the risk of mammary cancer, which is common in older entire females, and pyometra, which is a life threatening womb infection which can occur after a season.

Spaying prevents the bitch coming into season, which removes the risk of accidental mating.

Some female dogs can suffer from temperament changes during oestrogen and progesterone production. As this only occurs during and immediately after a season, spaying can have a positive stabilising effect.

For some bitches however, spaying may not be advisable. Neutering females that are nervous in temperament or showing aggressive tendencies, can potentially make the problem worse. Careful consideration should be taken in these cases.

Implications of Spaying Too Early

As with male dogs, it is inadvisable to neuter females before they are sexually mature.

The consequence of prepubescent spaying can be a life time of urinary incontinence, as the lack of oestrogen has a direct influence on the development of the sphincter muscles.

The only way to ensure that bitches have reached sexual maturity is to allow them to have their first season. The age at which this occurs varies from bitch to bitch. Generally this happens between the ages of 7 to 12 months although giant breeds can be much later.

The duration of the season is usually around three weeks. Once the season has finished, you should leave it at least 10 weeks before considering surgery. Bitches produce progesterone for the gestation period of a pregnancy, approximately 9 weeks, whether they are pregnant or not. Bitches should not be spayed during hormone production, as a sudden cut off can potentially cause long term behavioural complications.

My best advice is to read as much on the subject of neutering as possible and make the decision that you feel is right for your own dog.

.

- -

AND FINALLY...

It is my hope that the information contained in this book will help you train your dog effectively and build a deeper understanding and appreciation of your companion.

If we base our relationship with our dogs on understanding, consistency and a positive approach we are rewarded with loyalty, obedience and companionship for life, allowing us to truly appreciate the wonder and joy that dog ownership can offer.

If you can spare a few moments, I would really appreciate your feedback. Please consider leaving an honest review for this publication with your supplier.

But most of all... enjoy your dogs!

ABOUT THE AUTHOR

Karen Davison grew up in Bedfordshire, England. She has been both an avid reader and a lover of animals since early childhood. When she was eight, the family got their first dog Scamp, whose great character started Karen's lifelong devotion to dogs.

Since qualifying in Canine Psychology in 2001, she has worked as a professional dog trainer and canine behaviourist. She went on to study Wolf Ecology in 2009 and was lucky enough to spend time with the wolves at the UK Wolf Conservation Trust in Reading.

Her first publication, *The Perfect Companion: Understanding, Training and Bonding with your Dog*, a comprehensive guide to canine psychology, training and problem solving, was published in June 2012 and won an IndiePENdants' award for quality. Since then she has published *The Complete Guide to House Training Puppies and Dogs, Companion Huskies: Understanding, Training and Bonding with your Dog*, and three Fun Reads for Dog Lovers: *A Dog's Guide to Humans, A Dog's Guide to Cats* and *It Shouldn't Happen to a Dog Trainer*.

After joining a local writers group, she has spread her author wings and is now enjoying writing poetry, flash fiction and short stories, and after taking

- -

a course in screenwriting has just completed her first radio drama script.

She is currently working on her first work of fiction, which combines her love of writing, wolves and fantasy - *Wolf Clan Rising* which is due to be published 2018 under the pen name K.D. Phelan.. You can find an excerpt of Wolf Clan Rising at the end of this publication.

Karen is now living the dream, she resides in a country cottage on the west coast of Ireland, drawing inspiration for her writing from the peace and beauty of her surroundings where she shares her life with her husband, two daughters and nine special needs pets. Her seven rescue dogs and two rescue cats have a mixture of emotional, behavioural and physical disabilities

One of Karen's favourite sayings: 'Saving one dog will not change the world, but surely for that one dog, the world will change forever.'

Meet the author, join Karen on Facebook:-
https://www.facebook.com/SmartdogBooks

OTHER PUBLICATIONS
FUN READS FOR DOG LOVERS

A DOG'S GUIDE
TO HUMANS

A light-hearted look at the human species from a dog's point of view. Bob the Westie shares some tips on getting the best out of human beings, attempts to fathom some of their strange behaviour and imparts some wisdom on training and manipulation techniques.

A DOG'S GUIDE
TO CATS

Bob once again puts paw to paper. This time it's the old enemy... Cats.

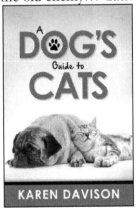

Don't be fooled by their apparent small stature and fluffy cuteness, these things have super powers that you can only dream of and their instincts are as sharp as their claws.

- -

IT SHOULDN'T HAPPEN TO A DOG TRAINER

During her career as a professional dog trainer, Karen Davison has been battered, flattened, tied up in knots and found herself in some funny, strange and painful situations.

Here she shares some of the 'you couldn't make it up' moments' that have occurred while working with dogs and their owners

POSITIVE DOG TRAINING SERIES

COMPANION HUSKIES

Based on the Perfect Companion with additional breed specific information for these high energy dogs.

Breed history, hereditary health problems, special dietary requirements and more.

COMPLETE GUIDE TO HOUSE TRAINING

Separate information booklet on house training puppies and dogs.

This information is now included in The Perfect Companion, Understanding, Training and Bonding with your Dog.

COMING SOON FROM SMARTDOG BOOKS

- -

WOLF CLAN RISING
Book One

K.D. PHELAN

The mage's dreams are haunted by a dark spirit. It moves through the forest, its limbs, tentacle-like and writhing turn everything to ash.

It is a warning but what does it mean?

Laya knows, she has seen it in a dream that is not a dream. There are strangers in the forest… and they are hunting the wolf.

And this is only the beginning… The invaders are taking over and they won't stop until they have stripped the land and enslaved its people.

A boy travels with them, born into slavery in a city far across the ocean; he had never questioned his fate, but the forest has stirred something deep inside him. Will he have the courage to betray his masters?

Can the clans prevail? Or is this the beginning of the end for the hunter-gatherers?

EXCERPT FROM WOLF CLAN RISING

Prologue

Excerpts from the diary of Edian Wright first officer of The Explorer.

Year 712, Moons 4th, Day 29

After many delays, we finally depart Lyconia. The excitement of starting our adventure is tinged with trepidation. We are going into the unknown.

The Emperor committed some of his own personal wood reserves into building this great ship, in the hope that we will discover a new land, rich in much needed resources.

If the bird experts are right, there is land out there somewhere, they have observed birds migrating south, disappearing from our shores for many moons. They must be heading somewhere.

Birds, it seems, are to be our guides. We have brought ravens with us to aid our search; we will release them periodically and from a higher vantage point their horizon will be far beyond ours. They are unable to land on water so if they return to ship, we will know that our search continues, if they spot land, we can track their course.

We have 163 souls on board consisting of 85 crew, 30 craftsmen, 45 slaves and 3 bird handlers. We leave on a prosperous wind on course South by Southwest.

Year 712, Moons 5th, Day 25

After six days, the storm has finally abated. Six of our crew lost overboard, good men all, and Petra's injuries are so bad, the Doc doesn't think he is going to make it.

The storms we had previously experienced navigating the shores around Lyconia pale in comparison to the ferocity and duration of storms out here in the midst of this vast ocean. At least for the time being the sea is calm, and we have made repairs as best we could.

There was great excitement among the bird handlers this morning when they caught sight of an unknown and impressively large seabird. I paused in my work to join them, and the sight of such a magnificent creature took my breath away. The wingspan was wider than the tallest of men, its flight pattern, they told me, was unlike anything they had every seen. It glided effortlessly, using the great expanse of its wings to harness the wind, as it rose and fell, turning and soaring above the waves.

Year 712, Moons 7th, Day 5

We have been away from port for three moons, rations are low and tempers short. We released a raven this morning, and hope surged as we watched it heading away from ship. We adjusted our course to follow, only to find a rocky outcropping, home to

- -

thousands of gulls, their raucous cries filling the air, their excrement turning the rocks white. This bitter blow pushed some of the crew over the edge, a fight broke out between two of the men and the Skipper put them both under the lash and cut their rations for two days.

Moral is at an all time low and there are murmurs of dissent. If we do not find land soon, I fear we will all die out here.

The Skipper still has us on a course South by Southwest.

Year 712, Moons 7th, Day 15

Late afternoon we spotted whales breaching the waves in the distance, and over the course of the day we saw patches of weed floating on the surface of the water, good indications that land may be nearby. At first light we will release the ravens again.

These latest sighting have given us some small hope and stirred in me a deep yearning. What I wouldn't give to feel land beneath my feet once again!

Year 712, Moons 7th, Day 16

The morning broke eerily calm, not a breath of wind to fill our sails, the creaking of timbers and the faint lapping of water against the hull the only sound in the thick sea mist that surrounded the ship, cutting us off from world.

It was mid morning before the sun and wind finally cleared it away and we were able to release one of the birds.

We watched as it circled the ship, gaining height and instead of returning, set off on a direct flight path two points off the starboard bow. The skipper ordered a course change and we followed. When we lost sight of it, we released another raven, until at last a great shout from the crow's nest of Land-Ho.

The rejoicing on board was something to behold, even the captain joined in the celebrations, breaking open his last barrel of malt spirit to share with the crew. There are no words to express the atmosphere of joy and excitement.

And what a land! It is more than we could ever have dreamed.

As we navigate its coast it appears uninhabited, with no signs of civilisation, a green jewel of rich forests and vast mountain ranges.

A land of plenty, a paradise.

Chapter One

The setting sun filters through the forest, casting golden rays that dance with the spirits of the living canopy. Through the dappled sunlight, a lone wolf moves on silent paws along the narrow trail, his powerful legs cover the ground at an easy trot.

Far to the north, the distant howls of stranger wolves carry to him faintly on the wind; he pauses, pricking his ears towards the sound. Licking his nose he inhales to explore his surroundings.

The north east wind brings with it the scent of snow from the high peaks and the freshness of the White Water river. Close by, rain and earth, the souls of trees, and spirits of a myriad living things that inhabit the forest. The wolf smells what is and also, what has gone before. The older scents are fainter, like the tracks of ghosts.

He registers this in a few heartbeats then lifts his muzzle and flaring his nostrils, casts his mind out further still, seeking the one scent that has caused such restlessness. The one that surrounds him, an invisible force that pulls him further and further away from his pack.

The scent of the she-wolf.

On the wind, a minute trace of what he seeks causes his heart to race. He lifts his head and raw emotion flows from his lips, quietly at first, rising and falling until the air is filled with a long and wavering howl. Caught by the wind, it travels through the forest.

Away to the south his own pack add their song, their voices weaving around his, wrapping him with warmth and comfort, and bringing with it an overwhelming sense of loss.

In the midst of the voices, he hears his soul brother calling to him. His chest tightens and for a moment he looks back over his shoulder but as twilight descends, the faint cry of the she-wolf beckons him north.

To receive notification when new titles are available, visit www.dogtrainingkerry.com and sign up for our newsletter:

Made in the USA
San Bernardino, CA
08 January 2018